LISTENING TO OUR TEACHERS

ALSO BY TORIN M. FINSER

School as a Journey
The Eight-Year Odyssey of a Waldorf Teacher and His Class (1995)

School Renewal
A Spiritual Journey for Change (1999)

In Search of Ethical Leadership
If not now, when? (2003)

Silence Is Complicity
*A Call to Let Teachers Improve Our Schools
through Action Research—Not NCLB* (2007)

Organizational Integrity
*How to Apply the Wisdom of the Body
to Develop Healthy Organizations* (2007)

Initiative
A Rosicrucian Path of Leadership (2011)

Finding Your Self
Exercises and Suggestions to Support the Inner Life of the Teacher (2013)

A Second Classroom
Parent–Teacher Relationships in a Waldorf School (2014)

Guided Self-Study
*Rudolf Steiner's Path of Spiritual Development:
A Spiritual-Scientific Workbook* (2015)

Leadership Development
Change from the Inside Out (2016)

Education for Nonviolence
The Waldorf Way (2017)

Parables (2018)

The False Door between Life and Death
Supporting Grieving Students, Teachers, and Parents (2019)

A Call to Teach
In Service of Waldorf Teacher Education and Lifelong Learning (2020)

Listening to Our Teachers

Advocacy through Research

Torin M. Finser, PhD

SteinerBooks | 2024

STEINERBOOKS
An imprint of Anthroposophic Press, Inc.
834 Main Street, PO Box 358, Spencertown, NY 12165
www.steinerbooks.org

Design: William Jens Jensen
Cover image: Fiddlehead fern spiral (photographer unknown):
*Research can be either a maze or a spiral. Whether personal
or academic, it can help us discover new layers of meaning.*

LIBRARY OF CONGRESS CONTROL NUMBER: 2024937771

ISBN: 978-1-62148-375-5

Table of Contents

Introduction   vii

1. Why Standardized Testing Is De-structive
   and Why Teacher Research Can Be Con-structive   1

2. The Cultural Life in Community   6

3. Opening a Space for Research: Questions   13

4. Perceptions of Obstacles to Teacher Research   16

5. Reinventing Research: New Concepts, New Approaches   20

6. Why Do Research?   24

7. Seeing, Feeling, Finding Your Question   31

8. Thoughts on Research Methods   35

9. Qualitative Research Design:
   The Five Essential Components   45

10. Organizing a Research Project   47

11. Ethical Consideration in Research   52

12. Learning from Indigenous Ways   54

13. Sharing Research   60

14. A Sampling of Recent Master's Projects:
    Advocacy through Research
    by Alison Henry, PhD   68

15. A Collaborative Model for Teacher Research:
    Building a Culture of Research in a School   74

16. Research and the Inner Life   81

17. Why Do Research? (Revisited)   92

18. The Uncertainty Principle in Research   98

19. The Use of AI for Teacher Research   99

20. Research as Teacher Empowerment   103

Appendices:

1. A Metaphor: Soulful Soup
    by Erin Geesaman Rabke   107

2. Kairos: Healing in a World of Need
    by Karine Munk Finser   111

3. World Social Initiative in Transition
    by Joan Sleigh   113

4. Alternative Question Formats   117

5. Fieldwork Strategies and Observation Methods   118

6. Interviews   119

7. Variety in Qualitative Inquiry: Theoretical Traditions   121

8. Typology of Research Purposes   122

9. Sampling Strategies   124

10. Design Issues and Options   126

11. Variations in Interview Instrumentation   128

    Notes   130

    Bibliography   132

Introduction

Starting with our Antioch Waldorf summer sequence program for experienced educators in 1992, I have taught courses at the university that introduce students to action research. That experience led to the publication of a small pamphlet on research brought out by the Association of Waldorf Schools in 1995. With the confluence of that original piece going out of print and subsequent invitations to speak at various conferences, I did some editing that ended up as a new pamphlet, *Silence is Complicity,* this time published by SteinerBooks. Now many years later, and with all sorts of changes in the educational landscape, this third version is appearing as *Listening to our Teachers: Advocacy through Research.*

Although some of the basic guidelines for teacher research remain the same in this version, there are several significant edits and additions.

Much of the discussion of No Child Left Behind (NCLB) has faded away, and although there are still many schools and children being left behind, the particular legislation of NCLB has been replaced by Common Core and other policies. In general, with this edition I am less interested in handwringing over governmental policy (although my concerns remain) and focused more on how our teachers can model the change we seek in public policy.

I have added chapters on research and the inner life, working with time, indigenous research methods and more. I hope the reasons for these additions become obvious as my readers turn the pages.

Since the Waldorf Program at Antioch University has continued its long tradition of supporting students doing original research, I have not only described their initial projects done early in the program, but have included, thanks to my dear colleague Alison Henry, a section on the masters and capstone projects done after all course work is completed.

What remains is my *basic case for teacher research:*

1. When conducted according to accepted quantitative or qualitative methods, doing research can help teachers learn, develop new curricula and stay enthusiastic about the discovery process. There are immediate, tangible benefits for both teachers and their students in action research.

2. When successful, teacher research can serve to empower teachers in their advocacy for educational change. With firsthand experience and earned knowledge, teachers can more confidently speak out for the needs of their students and schools. Those in other professions, such as medicine, engineering and business, are often afforded greater respect and compensation than teachers who have to endure countless commission reports and political debate about what others think should be happening in our schools. It would be great (for a change) if the voices of teachers were heard in our public discourse! They work with children every day; they know what materials and curricula are needed, if only they were left alone to follow their instincts. Teacher research takes this beyond intuitive understanding to a level

of documented inquiry that could be held up for public scrutiny, such as in publications, news media, workshops and town meetings. Teachers need a greater voice in educational matters!

3. Given enhanced curriculum and stronger advocacy on the part of teachers, we might achieve a third aim, which would be to get politicians to back off. No other professional field is so regulated and legislated as is education. Somehow, someone got the idea that in a democracy everyone has an equal say in educational matters. Yet when I go to the dentist or doctor, they are comparatively free to perform their work according to standards set by their professional organizations. I have yet to read a newspaper article describing legislation mandating a certain number of fillings per week before a dentist is publicly labeled as "failing." Yet we seem to have no problem letting politicians set very specific standards and test scores for our children. Teacher research, if followed as described in the book, could create a counter movement that would be so dynamic that parents and community members might band together in a popular revolt that essentially said: Listen to our teachers!

This will of course take time. But I sense that more and more people are willing to follow the lead of Jonathan Kozol (author of *Savage Inequalities* and other books) in challenging common malpractices in funding, testing and legislating. Most social change happens when people start to speak out and others rally to the cause. The time is right for such a new surge of educational reform.

Having coached countless students over the past thirty-five years with their Master-level projects and, having served on doctoral committees at several universities, I have been able to hone the techniques described here based upon life experience. Repeatedly, students and teachers have said to me that the research experience has been transformational. They have not only learned to become better teachers and stronger advocates for what they believe in, but they also feel their lives have changed as they follow a question that becomes a steady companion on the journey of teaching. Research is not just about outcomes and school reform. This is an opportunity for awakening, for inner development. In this regard, there are truly no limits to knowledge—no boundaries around personal growth.

1

Why Standardized Testing Is De-structive
and Why Teacher Research Can Be Con-structive

S ome of the most frequently voiced objections to standardized testing are as follows:

1. There is increasing evidence that schools are turning into test-prep factories and the curriculum offered as a result is narrowing. Along with this, teachers have less and less freedom in deciding on curriculum they know their students need.

2. In the pursuit of reading and math scores, the overall breadth and depth of the curriculum has diminished. Learning is being sacrificed at the expense of skill development.

3. The parental choice (and charter schools) can be helpful in support of innovation but should not come at the expense of supporting public schools that have been serving a community a long time.

4. The federal government has always had a hard time forcing states and local governments to do things they don't want to do, and even if they go through the motions, it's nearly impossible to force them to do those things well. As with children, they need support, resources and motivation to succeed.

5. Speaking of children, many teachers have reported that over-reliance on testing has reinforced a student's tendency to ask: Will this be on the test? Then they devalue

anything that is not. Ironically, some studies have shown (Popham 2006) that most of the tests are "unable to detect any striking instructional improvements when such improvements occur."[1]

6. In many cases, scores of marginalized student groups are not improving, and they are the ones most likely to be taught by inexperienced teachers with low salaries.

7. Abstract skills and subject area expertise is being pushed at the expense of a more integrated curriculum that corresponds to the real-life skills needed in the workplace.

8. The notion of "failing schools" is a form of public ostracism harking back to the "scarlet letter" condemnations that used public opinion as a punitive weapon. Embarrassment and ridicule do not promote growth and change.

The most significant question in my view concerns the very issue of the government's role in setting standards in the first place. As Mike Petrilli point out:

> In my opinion, the way forward starts with a realistic assessment of what the federal government can reasonably hope to achieve in education. Using sticks and carrots to tug and prod states and districts in desired directions has proven unworkable.[2]

He suggests the federal government's role should be restricted to distributing funds and collecting and publishing data, leaving everything else in the "don't do it at all" bucket: "No more prescriptive 'cascade of sanctions' for failing schools.... The states (should) worry about how to define and achieve greater teacher quality (or better, teacher effectiveness). The states (should) decide when and how to intervene in failing schools."[3]

One has to wonder if the same arguments Petrilli uses to question the federal government forcing unwanted changes on states should not be applied to states doing the same to local districts. Can excellence in education be legislated at all?

One crucial issue is the notion of setting standards and forcing schools nationwide to achieve them. Except for rare situations such as anti-trust issues, government does not do this for business, for if it did, entrepreneurship would seriously suffer. Imagine legislation that would mandate five percent profit margins for shoe stores or fifteen percent for technology companies, and then publicly brand companies as failures if they did not achieve these preset standards. As a society, we tend to value free enterprise and individual creativity in business but not in education, and we do this at our peril.

One of the main problems is setting standards in the first place. In her book *One Size Fits Few*, Susan Ohanian asserts that the Standardistos have de-professionalized teaching:

> How else are teachers to feel except helpless in the face of being told to *deliver* a curriculum that is invented by external authorities? Nationwide, we have the lowest retention rate of teachers in history.... What few people realize is that there is no *reform* in the Standardistos documents: Standardistos are trying to pass off macaroni and cheese skills as *Ziti con Formaggio Velveeta di Alfa Romeo* gourmet dining. They want to perpetuate the same old skill drill that kids have been resisting all this century.[4]

Teachers are caught in the bind between best practices known to most dedicated educators and the generalized arrogance of standards such as these issued by the Illinois State Board of Education:

Every elementary school child will be able to read at grade level, with fluency and comprehension.

Every elementary school teacher will be able to teach reading using comprehensive, research-based methods.[57]

And these and other standards are to be applied to all students regardless of their socioeconomic background, capabilities, developmental and learning differences, interests and ambitions. Are we considering DEI when designing and administering standardized tests? These standards are intended for students in districts with ample resources and those that can afford school supplies and lab equipment. The brush of standards tends to paint all schools with an unexciting, oppressive hue of gray. Real people otherwise known as children and teachers become numbers and charts. Standards set outside of the teaching profession are detrimental to all learning and creativity.

It is amazing, as stated previously, that only in education do people feel it legitimate to have outsiders set predetermined standards of achievement. Does the government legislate how many operations a surgeon should perform per week? Does anyone outside of the industry decide how many innovations a technology company should adopt in a given year? Did anyone require that Picasso produce a certain number of masterpieces a month demonstrating proficiency in certain techniques? The surgeon, painter or inventor relies upon the very human capacities that good teachers are trying to cultivate in our schools. These qualities include such things as imagination, critical thinking, problem solving, interpersonal skills, creativity—most of which are not valued or measurable on any standardized test. In focusing primarily on preset skill levels determined by outside authorities, we are sacrificing the very development of capacities that will shape our future and move us forward as a society. We are forfeiting future human capital in the test mills of today's classrooms.

Anyone who has ever worked in a classroom or has tried to understand child development knows that those who are closest to the children often have the best insights as to how to educate. Peggy Cooper, a past participant in our Waldorf Teacher Education Program at Antioch New England summer sequence program says:

> For me, the real heart of the process of research manifests itself in my everyday work with children. The in-depth reading can then lend support to my ongoing process as a teacher. Life is a constant state of becoming. When we do not work with the principle of continuous growth, we lose an important dynamic in our work with children, and we also run the risk of materialization of the spirit (dogmatizing something that should be an on-going process of maturation). Every day is a new opportunity to learn from our work. What I discovered in my research is that data gathered from a living process is a vital and valid way to sustain continuous research as a teacher.

Good teaching is a responsive activity; watching and observing the activities and interests of children leads to innovative lesson plans and creative group activities. Dedicated teachers are tired of being told what to do by people who do not understand the spirit of childhood. It is time to begin a new chapter in education by fighting for the emancipation of the teacher. And one way to empower teachers is to give them a chance to do research, share their findings, and advocate for change.

2

The Cultural Life in Community

More than six decades ago, John Fentress Gardner spoke words that are more relevant than ever:

> America today is dispirited. She is fast losing her vision and her confidence. She waits to be lifted. She longs to be renewed. But the only way for our country to open up a full draft of fresh inspiration is through coming closer again to spiritual insights and values! And this can be done for the nation as a whole only through education. But this opening up of the wellspring of what alone makes life worthwhile cannot be undertaken until a "wall of separation" has been raised between *school* and state similar to the one the First Amendment raised long ago between *church* and state. All schools must become independent schools.[6]

I would like to begin by distinguishing between "independent" and "private." Because of early initiatives in higher education in North America such as William and Mary College, Harvard, and others, the notion of private education took hold and was the exclusive domain of those who could afford such an education. Thanks to Horace Mann and others, public schools were eventually founded on the premise that education should be open to all. Without going into an extensive recapitulation of the history of American education, let us suffice to say that for over two hundred years we have had two strands, the one preserved as the Harvard legacy called private education and the other being our much-needed public schools. Even our university system has perpetuated this division into state universities and private colleges. Those included in the private sector are often more expensive and value selectivity, while those in the public realm value open access to all. These two currents run throughout our society, offering competing values of individuality vs. inclusion.

In my view, an "independent" school combines the values of both, in that such a school tries to serve "the public" by providing quality education to a diverse group of students while refusing to accept government mandates and testing requirements. An independent school is not necessarily made up of wealthy families, as most have active scholarship programs and enlist the parents in seeking broad community support through voluntary contributions. Most of all, independent schools value the insight of teachers in setting policy and the freedom of parents to select a school of their choice.

Thus, in his call for all schools to become independent, John Gardner did not mean privatization but rather freeing schools from state and federal control. The closest things we have today in this regard are the increasingly popular charter schools which are granted permission to operate, often with considerable freedom. However, testing and teacher licensure remain an issue in many cases.

The notion that the government should guide education is deeply ingrained in the mindset of most people today. Whenever we have a social challenge, we reflexively turn to state and federal governments for a solution, and it is hard to find new ways of working things out. I have witnessed some remarkable innovation in our public Waldorf schools (such as starting an aftercare program or new school lunch service at Golden Valley, CA), but these positive changes often come about because of remarkable people on the ground, on site. And for every innovation, hours are needed on compliance issues. It is one thing if handled as an administrative matter, hopefully with competent professionals on hand, but when teachers are required to devote more and more time on compliance matters it takes away from dedicated classroom work and the ever-growing needs of our children.

In 1919, Rudolf Steiner, the Austrian scientist and educator who started the Waldorf School in Stuttgart that year, spoke on behalf of the freedom of the teacher:

> One can only do one's work as an educator when one stands in a free, individual relationship to the pupil one teaches. One must know that, for the guidelines of one's work, one is dependent only on *knowledge of human nature,* the principles of social life and such things, but not upon *regulations or laws* prescribed from the outside.... The growing human being should mature with the aid of educators and teachers independent of the state and economic system, educators who can allow individual faculties to develop freely because their own have been given free rein.[7]

In order for this to take place, Steiner advocated for the complete disassociation of the educational system from government and industry: "The place and function of educators within society should depend solely upon the authority of those engaged in this activity. The administration of the educational institutions, the organization of courses of instruction and their goals should be entirely in the hands of persons who themselves are *simultaneously* either teaching or otherwise productively engaged in cultural life."[8] I myself have often discovered leadership success when the principal or faculty administrator has prior classroom experience and continues to interact with students, formally or informally.

Briefly stated, Steiner envisioned a reordering of the social life that would include three distinct spheres of activity, the "rights life" that is commonly understood as part of governance, the economic realm which includes the production and distribution of goods and services, and the cultural life. He felt that these areas needed to be distinct, even while interacting with one another, to allow the potential of each sphere of activity to manifest unencumbered.

What is meant by "cultural life?" Here one can include the Metropolitan Museum of Art in New York City, the local children's museum, the regional music or dance company, universities, schools and learning centers—any grouping of people who are dedicated to the development of human capacities. People in these groups participate out of a common vision and recognize talent in all forms. The key ingredient in these cultural groups is the free unfolding of human potential over time. The theatrical performance I attended a few nights ago may continue to influence me for days, even years to come. The value of what those professionals offered cannot be measured by the ticket price—in fact, the admission was actually just my voluntary contribution to their work. They gave me so much to discuss and remember. A good performance can nourish the soul. Indeed, many of these cultural institutions reach out to the community through enrichment programs with the schools to encourage attendance and participation.

The cultural sphere is distinct from the economic realm, which is dedicated to the creation of goods and services that support our human needs for living. If one stops to examine the shoe one is wearing, it quickly becomes apparent that many people contributed to the production, distribution, and sale of the shoe. In the economic realm we are inextricably bound up with our brothers and sisters all over the world. With the sphere of government which is meant primarily to promote the equal rights of all—no matter what status or degree one might hold—we each have the same essential right to clean water, fresh air, and basic governmental functions. Above all, we have the right to vote, and this ensures that each person is heard in regard to the common good. We need democratic processes for society to remain healthy! These three spheres—the cultural, economic and rights realm—all have a valid place in society.

The difficulty arises when one sphere infringes on another, thus stifling the human spirit. This happens, as mentioned earlier, when the government legislates standards for schools or micromanages business. But it also works the other way around; schools for profit, run by corporations, are likewise not a good idea, as education has a longer timeline than the profits of business. We do not see the true fruits of good teaching until someone is well into adulthood—or many years later. Finally, when business tries to infringe on governmental processes through lobbyists, special interests and expense-paid trips (from Congress to the Supreme Court), healthy governance is subverted. We need to establish stronger firewalls between the three spheres, between cultural institutions, business, and government. Only then will the three best serve human interests.

Over the past decade I have had the privilege of working with several public Waldorf schools hosting our CfA Building

Bridges Program. I have admired how their school leaders have become adept at compliance issues while still fighting for a rigorous Waldorf curriculum. It is possible to adhere to state charter laws *and* still offer a Waldorf curriculum *if*:

- The leadership is committed to the core principles of Waldorf as espoused by the Alliance and Association of Waldorf Schools of North America (AWSNA)
- The public Waldorf teachers are required to do Waldorf teacher education and supported financially in doing so
- There is a culture of collaboration and professional development within the school as a whole
- Teachers work actively with parents so that they are not just there by default (refugees from other schools) but also learn to "buy in" to Waldorf education
- There is a true partnership with other Alliance schools and teacher education institutes
- School leaders work with non-Waldorf administrators in their district and state to push back against intrusive regulations

One may ask, if the government stays out of the conduct of schools (or regulations are minimal), how can one ensure that there will be any standards, any level of accountability? Well, just as there are accreditation agencies that help universities adhere to their espoused standards, so, too, AWSNA has established accreditation teams staffed by current or former teachers. Some schools opt for dual accreditation, thus modeling the kind of networking that promotes self-reflection. This process helps schools monitor progress, so that independent schools can establish long-range plans, set goals and find resources to achieve them. The point of this approach is that *the profession itself* sees to accountability, not the government. Thus, when there are challenges, we can turn to people who understand the dynamics of the classroom. Decisions might be made more on the basis of insight rather than politics.

Independence in the cultural realm of education will only survive the test of time if teachers engage in vigorous professional development. One of the best ways to do this is classroom-based action research. In order to achieve and maintain high standards in education, we need to look more closely at the ways in which teachers can actively participate in classroom research that would then be subject to peer review. Janey Newton, who participated in the Waldorf Teacher Education Program at Antioch University, explains how this manifested for her:

> The activity of engaging ourselves in individual research projects brings a real liveliness to the study of Anthroposophy and Waldorf education. When a topic such as the wisdom of fairy tales is researched, put into practice, and shared among colleagues, it gains a strength that it didn't have before. The kernels of truth that have been lifted from the research on practical applications can be planted in other Waldorf classrooms and life situations. This idea of shared research is much like reseeding the garden each year so that it will continue to flourish.

In the following chapters I will demonstrate that responsible research can renew the curriculum, raise standards, and enhance teacher learning without the imposition of external mandates and standards.

3

Opening a Space for Research: Questions

Teachers the world over have questions about their work, about the children they teach, lessons, materials, and the functioning of schools as organizations. These questions are real; they come from participation in the living stream of education. However, are these questions given a chance to resound in the cacophony of demands on teachers today? How can we make space for true questions arising from classroom practice?

In striving to meet the needs of children, Waldorf teachers become good at observation. They look at temperaments and learning styles, social interactions, handwriting, walking, speaking and drawing (not just academic performance). These observations are often child specific, yet they relate to the age group in general. Many of these observations provoke insights that can be helpful to other teachers. Can we find ways to share these child-centered observations beyond the faculty circle in one particular school?

Many teachers become unofficial librarians. They collect science materials, poems, songs, stories, skits, circle activities, math activities, student literature, and plays until, after some years, a teacher may possess a veritable treasure trove of materials. Within a school, there is often considerable sharing. Waldorflibrary.org and Waldorf Books have grown over the years and have served many teachers. Beyond these collections there are the gems, primary resources developed by teachers with special creativity and insight that are never published. I am speaking about original work, the creative stories, plays, activities and lessons that were created in a burst of enthusiasm in response to a particular challenge or classroom situation. How can we foster and expand this creativity?

By the very nature of their tasks, teachers follow a path of inquiry. Yet the focus often shifts from week to week and block to block depending upon immediate demands. It is understandably so hard to lift one's gaze above the many, many pressing daily needs of the classroom (not to mention the rest of one's life). Overwork can almost become addictive—we are so used to stress that, like caffeine, our physical/psychological constitution starts to exhibit a strange sort of dependency on continued stress. More than ever, we need self-care, healing modalities and new approaches to work/life balance. For years, Kim John Payne has worked in this sphere, as has Kairos at Center for Anthroposophy.

As indicated several chapters ahead, research is more than just another "project" to put on a to-do list. If the coaching is successful, finding one's question and taking time "away" to do contemplative work can nourish the soul. When we work from the core of our soul, pursue new learning, and find excitement and joy in discovery, we are nourished. Rather than taking time off (or leaving the profession) teachers need to find new sources of inspiration and new modalities of working. But it starts from the inner resolve to change the status quo.

To make this happen, we need to focus and organize our research efforts, and now more than ever. Bethany Craig, an alum from the Waldorf Teacher Education Program at Antioch builds on this theme:

Research is essential for the carpenter as well as for the teacher as well as for the philosopher. In order to work at the highest level possible, it is necessary to equip oneself with the best tools. But the question of research goes beyond the act of acquiring information. Life is a continual flow. In order to offer something, work, thoughts, whatever, to the world and to society, there must be an incoming flow to the doer and this is research whether of a factual or spiritual nature. It is food for humanity.

In beginning to work with some of the questions raised in the above paragraphs, the sections that follows will look at some of the obstacles common to classroom research, possible goals and methods, working with a question, and organizing and sharing. One section will describe a possible collaborative model for teacher research, and then also the spiritual/meditative aspects. Another chapter will look at some of my recent research on indigenous methodologies and the broader pedagogical implications of researching. This is not an exhaustive study on research. The aim is to stimulate inquiry, discussion, and the practice of research to renew our schools.

4

Perceptions of Obstacles to Teacher Research

In speaking with practicing teachers, three constraints are repeated again and again: time, resources and support. Here are the voices of a few public-school teachers considering research:

> Teachers seem to need more free time for research and for renewal. I wish schools could recognize this and somehow provide periods of time for professional work...perhaps floating teachers would help.

> Consider the economic and political implications of such research. What (administrative) entities have a vested interest in squelching it?

> Time, support, recognition of teachers as professionals and as people with expertise.... The daily stress and demands right now are too much. We can't add more to teachers' lives. We must be able to incorporate research into present teaching.... Less would lead to more, more opportunities for meaningful research.

> Please consider our current time and isolating constraints. How can we convince the wider community and administrative leaders that we need time and each other—for the benefit of the children?

The nature of the challenge may vary depending on each school, but the general themes emerging from independent Waldorf and public-school teachers are remarkably similar. Any effort to enhance teacher research will by necessity have to take full account of the obstacles they face.

But looking squarely at the challenges also provides an opportunity to re-conceive, re-design and re-think traditional assumptions about research. We need to reframe what we consider to be research—a point developed more fully in the next chapter—and start to see teacher research as an extension of learning (and living). Over the years I have found that if I simply "adopt" a question or theme for a while, I start to collect materials, meet people, have ideas, and over time a new project emerges. One need not take a year off from work to focus learning—it can be part of daily living. However, any research effort by practicing teachers needs to begin with an understanding of the following points:

1. A teacher's primary task is to teach. Any research needs to enhance teaching if it is to be meaningful both to the teacher and to the children.

2. It would be naïve to postulate that research does not consume a commodity in short supply, namely time. So rather than adding another layer of work onto the teacher's day, how can research actually enhance the quality of teaching and thus potentially save time in the end? If one can describe a situation in which preparation is facilitated and relationships within the school strengthened through research, one might be able to justify allocating some precious time for research. But for practicing teachers, the results need to be practical and viable if research is to be sustained over time.

3. Methods used in such research will need to be in harmony with the demands of the classroom and the school day. Thus, my main objective in the chapter on "methods" will be to demonstrate just how many possibilities are available for valuable research. One does not need to spend hours in the library to arrive at findings that may enhance education in more than one classroom.

4. If these findings are to have value beyond the classroom of one particular teacher, we will need to find ways of sharing information that go beyond the traditional route of scholarly publication. Teacher research is meant to be shared and used.

5. The above points translate into a bias toward qualitative research rather than traditional quantitative research.

Melissa McCall explains this point from her participation at Antioch:

> As I mulled over this question, I realized that, as an avid reader and quester, I've been engaged in a lifelong research project. Yet, in my work of delving into the wisdom of fairy tales this past year, I noticed a real shift in lifestyle. Though I only scratched the surface of this rich topic, the changes came in my whole attitude. "I'm doing research," I often found myself reporting proudly to anyone who would listen. Being in this mode meant that I was able to digest and articulate the material in a living way.
>
> Knowing that my Antioch peers were similarly engaged was a great source of strength during the intense research period. I intend to take up a new research project (on the Sophia) in September. I'm interested in hearing more about collaborative research.

As the author Glenda Bissex said when she gave a guest presentation during my course on educational research: "Quantitative research seeks to prove something; qualitative research seeks to learn something."

Teacher research is all about learning.[9]

5

Reinventing Research: New Concepts, New Approaches

As an experiment, I asked a group of people to give me a string of words that come to mind when hearing the term *research*. They brainstormed as follows: library, footnotes, readings, communication, scary, deadlines, interviews, dry, stressful, graphs, bibliographies, hypothesizing, notes, data, variables, control groups, stilted—to name only a few. Of course, I was surprised to hear that most of these words described traditional approaches to research. No wonder teachers have found little time for such work.

If research means to look again and again, to be open to the unknown in the search for new meaning, then perhaps we need to begin with a new characterization of "research" itself. Traditional research, by the way, is not really that open to the unexpected, since the hypothesis anticipates an answer, and the data collected is supposed to be solid enough to constitute "proof." Yet if one does a survey of the history of scientific research, for instance, one quickly realizes how soon the conclusions of one year are submerged by the totally new discoveries of the next. Besides, in the case of teachers, proof is often less important than learning—their own and especially their students' learning. As stated by David Hopkins, "Teachers and researchers do not conceptualize teaching the same way. They live in different intellectual worlds and so their meanings rarely connect...the usual form of educational research, the psycho-statistical or agricultural-botany paradigm, has severe limitations as a method of construing and making sense of classroom reality."[10] Thus teachers need a different approach to research if it is to have practical value.

In redefining "research" we can begin by illustrating our goals. For teachers, these might include:

1. Rather than serve mainly as a means of gathering information, research for teachers can be a vehicle for gaining understanding.[11] This means formulating your own questions, selecting a method that works for your results, which may not change the world but might very well change an aspect of your own teaching. Research for understanding involves a search for meaning rather than proof.

2. Being prepared for the unexpected requires an open mind and heart, as well as a willingness to be surprised. Rather than an emphasis on control, teacher research needs to be flexible and varied. We will discuss this further in the chapter on methods. As Ann Sauer states from her own experience through the Waldorf Teacher Education Program at Antioch, "The idea of doing educational research sounded somewhat dreadful until the actual midpoint of my first project. By then I had done enough reading, interviewing and observing that exciting correlations were forming. Questions arose that I lived with as I continued looking into the literature and observing children. The actual paper writing was a renewal and portal for future research. I learned that research creates faculties we may use for greater understanding of our children." This example of direct

experience along with other observations convinces me that this attitude of open-mindedness has spiritual and pedagogical value in itself, even if nothing else is "accomplished" in the research process.

3. These qualities of openness and flexibility do not negate the need for the discipline of inquiry. Once a question is identified and articulated, one goal is to follow its path with consistency and true discipleship. If it is one's own question that one is following, if one fully owns it, the systematic line of inquiry will be less onerous.

4. This leads to another goal: teacher research must be driven by burning interest. If one is not interested enough in a question to live with it for many months, find another one. *The research question needs an element of passion in order to be a long-term companion.*

5. Since teachers spend most of their time in action, doing things in the classroom with children, teacher-driven research needs to be action based. "Put simply, action research is the way groups of people organize the conditions under which they can learn from their own experience."[12] Action research can involve four phases: planning, acting, observing and reflecting. Much of this can be done in the classroom while teaching.

6. A final goal of teacher research involves the word *commitment*. Oh, how much is perpetrated in the name of this word! Yet, if research is to take hold in our schools, we need teachers who are committed to a path of inquiry. Given the constraints on time and energy, I suggest a research commitment to a small question, something that might seem insignificant at first. For

instance, rather than take a theme such as "How do children respond to mathematics when taught through movement in grades one to five?" the teacher might begin with something that has clear parameters: "Are children more attentive on Monday mornings if the day begins with math-movement activities?" Make a commitment to something that can be completed. Above all, make sure that the question selected directly relates to the rest of your teaching life. Judith Selin's experience at Antioch illustrates this point well:

> To devote time that allows immersion into research is a gift to oneself. It is also a beginning in many ways. To begin with the whole of the universe and its mysteries, to take one idea from it, to develop and explore it, to find its connections to the whole—in this, we find understanding, growth and confidence. We feel more empowered by our understanding and realize that this can be a beginning, a way for us to see the world one piece at a time.

6

Why Do Research?

In *Teacher Research*, Karen Ernest describes her experiences creating a community of learning, a group of teacher researchers. Afterward, she asked the teachers to review their work together. The participants felt that the project had affected their classroom work in the following ways: "Increased sense of professionalism; increased support for their own work through participation in a community of colleagues; support for changes in what or how they teach; awareness and practice in observation and reflection on their classroom; sense of empowerment to answer questions, challenge the status quo; and suggestions for change in teaching practice."[13]

This summary statement prompts a more detailed examination of the benefits of teacher research and why this activity should be pursued more vigorously. What follows are some of the most frequently cited reasons based on the literature I have reviewed.

The Performance Gap

A growing body of research suggests, first, that there is often incongruence between a teacher's publicly declared philosophy of beliefs about education and how he or she behaves in the classroom. Second, there is often incongruence between the teacher's declared goals and objectives and the way in which the lesson is actually taught. Third, there is often a discrepancy between a teacher's perceptions or account of a lesson and the perceptions or account of other participants (e.g., pupils or observers) in the classroom (Vide, Elbaz 1983). All of these discrepancies reflect a gap between behavior and intention and are a source for classroom research problems.[14]

Thus, this gap between what is and what could be then becomes a rationale for collaborative research. One might say that the kind of research model proposed in this book— a regional linkage of schools around research conferences and other suggestions—could help reduce the gap between perception and reality. Research is a means of self-evaluation and professional feedback.

Professional Development

It follows that teacher-directed research is likely to enhance teaching practices as the participant engages in a process of questioning, observing, refining, and reshaping attitudes and opinions. This process of personal growth and change can have a liberating effect on the profession as a whole. In recent years, state governments have imposed a web of restrictions and controls on public schools and have occasionally even ventured into the domain of private education. The public in general seems to continually demand more accountability from teachers and clearly defined educational "outcomes." How can teachers respond to these demands? One way is to emphasize more internal accountability, to establish standards and goals based on teacher-driven research findings, and not those of local politicians, thereby reclaiming freedom in culture and education. "By adopting a research stance, teachers are liberating themselves from the control position they so often find themselves in."[15]

Increased public scrutiny can thus become an opportunity to emphasize professionalism rather than arbitrary criteria such as the norms set by standardized tests. Teachers can assert leadership in their profession by shouldering more responsibility for their actions and creating a dynamic, creative learning environment through research.

Teachers as Role Models

Children learn not only through what is presented but also by how the teacher goes about his or her own process of learning. Someone who is eagerly pursuing a theme in research will provide a role model for the children even if the subject itself is not shared in the classroom. Teacher research feeds the children; for, as described at the end of this book, when a teacher's ego intensifies its work on the lower members, this transformative activity can enhance the quality of all teacher/child interactions. Thus, rather than being a cold, cerebral activity, research can actually increase the intimacy of relationships.

Building Professional Learning Communities

Numerous studies have shown that children learn better when they experience the adults around them as part of a professional learning community. This can mean both their teachers and their parents.

Do teachers meet regularly to share insights, curriculum study, child observations, their own research? Do parents participate in discussion groups on shared interests? When answered in the affirmative, these areas can stimulate enhanced learning by our students!

Shared Values

In the citation that began this section, the teachers used the word "support" several times in a few lines. Usually, one thinks of research as a lonely activity, something that might only increase a sense of alienation and separation from the rest of the world as one sits in the local library. Yet an action-research model could become just the opposite. If one works as a team within the faculty, engages in classroom research with the students as collaborators, and shares the results with colleagues on a regular basis, one can accentuate the school as a community of learners with shared goals. This process can be sustaining and deeply encouraging.

Observation

The following story told by Michael Patton, celebrated author on qualitative research, illustrates the power of observation when one is open to what the world has to teach, as well as the inductive analysis to extract meaning from simple phenomena that may have escaped the attention of other people:

> The story of the invention of modern running shoes illustrates these principles. The design of sneakers varied little until the 1960s, when competitive runners began to turn to lighter-weight shoes. Reducing the weight of shoes clearly improved performance, but problems of traction remained. A running coach, Bill Bowerman, went into the sneaker business in 1962. He paid close attention to the interest in lighter-weight shoes and the problems of traction. One morning while he was making waffles, he had an idea. He heated a piece of rubber in the waffle iron to produce the first waffle-shaped sole pattern that became the world standard for running shoes. Subsequently engineers and computers would be used to design and test the

best waffle patterns—but the initial discovery came from paying close attention, being open, making connections, drawing on personal experience, getting a feel for what was possible, exploration, documenting initial results, and applying what he had learned.[16]

As long as we focus only on what we expect to see, we are functionally blind. To quote Glenda Bissez again, "The world around us is a text, and we have stopped being able to read much of it. We listen to the weather report rather than looking at the sky."[17] Research can bring us out of the realm of weather reports and connect us with the sky, the primordial expanse of real learning through observation.

All teachers rely on secondary materials, source books, curriculum guides, lessons from other teachers, but do we have enough primary sources? *It would be very healthy for our schools as cultural institutions if we once dared to throw out all the accumulated materials from other people and had to teach from direct observation of our students' needs.*

Any research question based on classroom/school life, no matter how limited in scope, has the potential of sharpening our skills in observation that could then apply to a wide range of other activities. For example, observing how the children learn on Monday mornings before and after gross motor movement activities would heighten the teacher's awareness of student responses throughout the week. Teacher research is needed not only for the specific findings that may arise, but also for the all-important byproducts, such as a change in teacher consciousness. Once one really observes, one cannot stop. Research through observation becomes a healthy habit.

As a side remark, I would like to draw a small yet vital distinction between observation and inference. As Ted Sizer states in *Horace's Compromise*, "Everyday experiences show how important this distinction is. SAT scores have gone up two points. Some then hypothesize that because SAT scores have gone up, high schools must be getting tougher. The first statement is an observation, and the second a conclusion (of substantial dubiousness) drawn from the observation. Sloppy people confuse the two."[18]

Social Change

Any meaningful teacher research has the potential to effect social change. One has only to read Paulo Freire's *Pedagogy of the Oppressed* to experience a vivid, anguished example of how educational emancipation goes hand in hand with social and political change. I can imagine a path of social/political emancipation as follows:

> Teacher research as intense professional/spiritual striving can lead to
>
> An enhanced professional "voice" for teachers, which can lead to
>
> Strong, vibrant schools that serve as cultural centers, which can lead to
>
> Freedom for education and necessary restrictions on political and economic intrusions on cultural endeavors in general, which may result in a reconfiguration of the social organism.

Barbara Bedingfield's comments on her participation in the Waldorf Teacher Education Program at Antioch New England are a clear example. "My research, centered on the topic of child observation, helped me to deepen my understanding of the child as she unfolds during each developmental stage and to look with *new* eyes in a comprehensive way at every child.

Knowledge led to interest and interest to love, a love, I trust, that will guide me in my work with children."

So, if one considers the above points valid reasons for engaging and supporting classroom research, one then has to start looking at the beginning of the process, finding the questions or focus of study.

7

Seeing, Feeling, Finding Your Question

We all ask questions, of others and ourselves, all the time. These questions are varied and often not even verbalized. Some of our questions are factual in nature and are answered immediately: "Do I turn left on Hickory Street? How much does this watermelon cost?" Other questions stay with us for a while: "How come, whenever I sit down to work at my desk I get a text or call on my iPhone?" There are also questions that become companions, questions that remain with us for an extended period of time: *How can I achieve greater wholeness in my life and balance work and life?* The first questions mentioned often get the most daily attention, while the last ones often live under the surface far too long. So, it is these that are my focus in this section.

Traditional research suggests that you begin with a problem, hypothesis or specific topic. Yet for many teachers it is easier to begin with something more open ended, something that only indicates a direction of inquiry at first, such as:

> I would like to improve the...
> Some people are unhappy about...
> What can I do to change the situation...?
> I am perplexed by...[19]

My preference is to find a question rather than a problem and to do a series of "wonderings": I wonder how... I wonder about... I wonder if... To identify yours, you might make a long list in a stream of consciousness manner, then go back and find groupings, those that involve your class, the material, relationships, etc. When you have found your family of questions, try and formulate one question that speaks to the core issue.

Then try out your question on others. When I taught a workshop on educational research in Ann Arbor, Michigan, some years ago, I asked participants to write their question at the top of a blank page and pass it to the person on the left. We each had to react to the question in front of us. Some of the responses to the questions from those who received them were along these lines:

What do you really mean? This is not clear. Alternative phrasing could be: Have you considered...? This is really three issues.... You might call so and so... and so on.

Then we passed the pages to the next person, and so our questions made the rounds, receiving in all twenty-two responses. When our own questions had been returned to us after this "round robin" exercise, I asked that the feedback be considered overnight before we had small-group meetings and individuals wrote up a fully formed question for research. Most of the students in the class felt that this exercise was extremely helpful in terms of clarifying their thinking and that it also served as a validation of their issue and personal needs.

It is also possible to begin the research process without a clearly defined question. Here is another pearl from Glenda Bissex: "One thing that I've learned from myself as an observer is how I can unearth or excavate my own questions by following my own observations. What attracts my attention as I observe and what I find myself recording is information to help me answer questions that I may not yet have consciously asked."[20] Thus the process of finding a question and learning from it is a spiritual process that will be considered again in other sections of this book.

Jon Wagner, author of "Ignorance in Educational Research," speaks of how research can be designed to fill in "blank spots" in terms of questions already formulated and when one simply needs more information, or how research can provoke new questions that illuminate "blind spots" in existing theories, methods and perceptions.[21] Both avenues help us see the phenomena before us more clearly than before.

Harry Wolcott, another resource for the teacher-researcher, is attracted to the idea "of thinking about research as problem setting, rather than problem solving."[22] This consideration is helpful because teacher-researchers might inadvertently set themselves up for failure if they expect to solve all their "problems" through research. It is important to remember that success and failure can only be judged in relation to what you set out to do. Therefore, don't bite off more than you can chew. Finding questions, formulating problems and key issues is in itself a worthy act in the research process. As with the Grail Mystery and the story of Parcifal, the educator might be content to plead: May I be so *present* that, if nothing else, I learn to ask the right questions!

Finally, this quotation from Sandra Ruggiero, a participant in the Waldorf Teacher Education Program at Antioch, shows us one result that an open approach to research can have. "Doing research gives one an opportunity to delve into something with a depth that life seldom allows for in this day and age. It can be a counterpoint to balance the alacrity and shallowness of our other daily demands and pressures. To carry a question into waking and sleeping and through transformations of your own thinking is almost a form of meditation. To write it down is to allow others to also drink from the deep waters of your refreshing pool."

Having now served as a coach and mentor for countless research projects over three decades, I am deeply grateful for the many striving students like Sandra who discovered the deeper undercurrents of research. When a student finds her question through an extensive process of winnowing, group discussion, reflections over many nights, it can become a spiritually transformative force. When one can truly *recognize how a question finds us, it is like hearing the call of destiny. Listening to that call is no longer an option, it becomes a necessity as strong as the need for food and drink. A question can find us—and we find ourselves in following the beckoning call of our question!*

8

Thoughts on Research Methods

B efore delving into specific suggestions on methodology, I would like to share a few reflections in general. The most significant discovery I made in my own research efforts was that much can be discovered by using what is already at hand. One does not need to get on a plane, send away for all sorts of material, or run up a long phone bill in doing research. It is best to start with whatever happens to be readily available: the classroom, colleagues, parents, the students' work, and a literary search at the local library. By typing in a few key words, one gets a deluge of articles and citations for any given topic, not to mention what happens by just Googling. It is possible that one might even save that plane ticket for the "last round" of the research, when one is thoroughly familiar with the subject and can make the best use of an exotic visit. To modify a popular bumper sticker, *research locally, think globally.*

Also, it is important to sound another theme at this early stage: consider those who are being researched (see chapter on indigenous research methods). It is part of the abstract, some might say Western tradition in research to delve in, collect the data one wants, and not consider the process from the point of view of those who are being observed. I suggest that, at each stage and with each method, consider "how it feels" from the other end, trying whenever possible to use nonintrusive methods of data collection. For example, instead of bringing in your iphone video camera to observe social interactions (especially intrusive in a Waldorf classroom), try looking at carpet wear, listening to the children's comments, even examining the trash basket at the end of the day. Moreover, in an interview, it is not just the teacher who will be learning. Prepare a few questions but leave time for those comments or questions that may arise from the person being interviewed. The interview could also be considered a conversation. As one advisor in my doctoral program said, leave room for the unexpected in the interview conversation. (See the appendix for interviews and types of research.) Moreover, record your contributions in the discussion, because you may say something in the context of the interview to a particular person that would not have been possible if you had stuck to a straight question/answer format. In other words, you might discover something through the act of speaking.

Finally, by way of introductory comments, use triangulation. The suspicion concerning qualitative research has often been that it will be "soft" and unreliable. This makes triangulation all the more significant in terms of your credibility. Briefly put, triangulation involves using three or more means to answer the same question. Thus, if you want to find out how a child is sleeping at night:

1. Ask them casually when greeting in the morning—observe them in class
2. Interview their parents
3. Send your parents an email questionnaire to be completed daily over the course of a week
4. At a parent conference, ask the parents to go over the results with you and facilitate a conversation on sleep and learning

The fourth step is one of my favorites. It again takes research out of the "learned scholar realm" and makes it a community event. You can never really know all the facts, yet after collecting some data, you are open to reviewing it with those who gave their time to help you. It also serves as a convenient way to correct mis-impressions and possible bias on the part of the researcher. In real life, research is not a matter of data entry, but really a "spiraling in" toward greater understanding. Take your participants along on the journey.

What follows is not a list of methods to use, but rather an array of possibilities. Some may be more suitable for one given project than another. The element of freedom arises when one overcomes one's natural inclinations and tries a variety of techniques. (For another time and place: more than ever, the humans on this planet today need to put greater effort into overcoming subjectivity and striving, collectively, for greater objectivity that might approach something we call truth.)

Specific methods to consider for teacher research

1. *Be Awake in the Moment.* As stated above, use the classroom. Examine daily routine, the flow of the lessons, student responses and the many daily interactions *in the light of your question.* There is much that can be found in the ordinary.

2. *Field Notes.* Buy yourself a new binder with loose-leaf pages. Keep it on your desk in the classroom. In the morning, before the children arrive, reformulate your question at the top of the page, and enter the date (still prefer this over making notes on a tablet or iPhone as it is more classroom friendly). Then, during the school day, make short entries; incomplete sentences are fine for this

exercise. At the end of the day or in the evening, make additions that were not possible while in the middle of things. Use descriptions, and do not worry if things do not agree with each other. This method of taking field notes *helps focus you on the issue over time*, and it is good for general impressions and descriptions that can later be interpreted.

3. *Audio Recordings*. Most Waldorf teachers discourage use of electronic devices in the classroom with young children, and for good reason. Yet there are ways to work with recordings that I have found invaluable and should at least be considered in certain circumstances. Earlier I used to use a small tape recorder (I had one the size of my appointment book) that could be kept between two books on my desk. Likewise, an iPhone can be turned on to record for brief periods, and then erased after listening to it in the evening. It is particularly useful for one-on-one interactions, less helpful when there is a lot of background classroom activity. Vivian G. Paley wrote many of her books by simply recording her students in dialogue! Listening to a video recording later can help us hear with greater accuracy than in the moment and find nuances we had previously overlooked. *Of course, any recording or use thereof needs the permissions of those involved!*

4. *Video Recording*. This method is used increasingly in public schools and even teacher education programs. It is certainly intrusive, and I would not use it with young children. (The same is true with some of the constant use of cameras at some of our assemblies and class plays.) Yet if working with older students, colleagues, parents or a

community event, this method might be helpful in one's research, as one can view the interview or interaction again and again. Also, when one sees oneself in the video, it can promote a re-examination of gestures, movements and interpersonal interactions. Since covid, the use of zoom has greatly enhanced the opportunities to do recordings which can then be looked at again by the teacher doing research—it is amazing how much one sees in a second or third viewing.

5. *Pupil Diaries.* In many schools, students are asked to keep a journal or daily log at one grade level or another. This practice can double for teacher research, in that your assignment to them might include an aspect that you are investigating. Since you will be checking their work anyway, this method of teacher research is highly time efficient. Likewise, the student journal entries provide a stimulating counterpart to one's own fieldwork (#2 above).

6. *Questionnaires.* More appropriate for older students and certainly adults, this method allows you to ask very specific questions of many people. There are so many ways to do surveys these days, and Survey Monkey and others are easy to set up. The tool selected can collate as you go, or if done still with paper copies in a meeting, someone other than you can later collate the information if you are pressed for time. I am a big believer in research assistants—an intern, parent volunteer, etc. Using a scale of one to five is simpler, but sometimes open-ended questions yield more in-depth material. I suggest the teacher-researcher personally read the open-ended responses, for often things are said "between the lines." One tip: Do a

trial run of the survey first and then rewrite your questions based on any misunderstandings on wording. It is amazing how many ways a simple question can be understood. You want feedback from a few people so as to make your mistakes on a small scale before distributing the questionnaire to the masses. Also, it is not just the responses to specific questions that are of interest to the researcher, but the correlation of responses. You might even formulate the same question in different ways at various points in the survey.

A survey allows you to cast a broad net and involve many people in your work. I advise my Antioch students to use this method early on in a research project, as it also helps to identify issues and people for subsequent interviews.

7. *Case Studies.* "A case study is individual research in a small context. We may not know enough based on our individual classroom case studies to know which are the generalizations that will hold true for other teachers. But other teachers will know. As teacher researchers, we can't make those generalizations, but they will be made by our readers. I believe our classroom case studies can offer valuable insights for other teachers, but the basis for those insights is not generalizations, but universals, which is also what makes literature endure. The things we have in common as human beings—those fundamental things that we have in common as teachers—are going to be there, in those case studies or pieces of literature. They endure because they continue to speak to what is fundamental in human experience, or in teaching experience."[23]

I found in my research that case studies were like writing a biography. I really got to know the people I worked with. After using some of the above-mentioned methods, it was also refreshing to go into depth and explore issues with someone over time. We especially need more longitudinal studies of children as they progress through the grades. The case study informs and compliments the material gathered by other means.

8. *Documentary Evidence*. This sounds like the work of a detective, or perhaps Ken Burns, but it is actually one of the most readily available methods for Waldorf teachers. Our students create a wealth of material: main lesson books, compositions, drawings, paintings, homework assignments and projects. All this becomes fodder for the researcher, if the eye is trained to observe. This means not just living in the moment with the child as the work is created, but afterward stepping back and *seeing it again* with the eye of a researcher. When I wrote *School as a Journey*, each evening I spread out my students' work from that grade, viewed it with "beginner eyes," and then went to sleep. Upon waking, I looked again and then write that grade-level chapter.

If nothing else, write your research question in big letters and stand it up on your desk. Then take a pile of the children's creations and look at each one in light of your inquiry. You will be amazed at what can be found.

And just a note on the healing modalities: viewing children's drawings and paintings can reveal much of the soul life of a child, if we are trained to observe as in the case with TSHE and Kairos classes offered through Antioch and Center for Anthroposophy.

9. *Peer Observation*. We often do not visit each other's class-rooms enough. One way to build community in the school is to share resources and do research. Schedule a series of peer visits to your classroom. Give your visitor a notebook with your questions or issues on the cover and ask him or her to observe your lesson with these in mind. Be sure to have the follow-up conversations needed. Much may have been observed that you missed. Take notes during the dialogue. Write them up and a few days later share them with the colleague who visited. This kind of research method helps create a circle of care.

10. *Critical Incidence Research*. We all know about those unexpected "happenings" that occur from time to time in schools. Use them. If an incident occurs on the playground between two children, observe and record exactly what transpires as it may in fact speak to larger issues that live in the social fabric of the class. Or take a series of incidents in one class over time and look at them. How did you respond? What was revealed? The critical incident is like a moment of wakefulness that can shed light on the larger picture.

11. *Interviews*. Already mentioned above, I would simply like to add that one needs to be aware of the types of questions one asks (see appendix). For instance, certain kinds of questions will prompt dichotomous responses such as Yes, No, Yeah, Sort of, and so on. Open-ended questions tend to draw a person out. Sometimes one might even want to ask questions that have a lead-in or presupposition such as: How effective do you think the foreign language program is at this school? Here you

are presupposing that the person interviewed can make a judgment about the program. Clarity of intent on your part is essential if the interviews are to be successful. Know the difference between what, how, when and why questions.

In addition to the usual type of interviews you might conduct, there are third-party interviews that you may not have considered: classroom observer/student, student/student, and observer/observer. You can facilitate the gathering of data without always being at the center of the action.

When I did my PhD, a member of my committee suggested I select a relaxed place to do interviews, such as around a kitchen table or at a coffee shop, and that I should treat the interviews as a conversation. This has implications for unexpected learning, and I have found that the "external conversation' is often matched by an "internal conversation" within me that runs parallel. Sometimes I have even recorded the one aspect on the left side of my note pad and the other on the right side. Many "ah-ha" moments have occurred while swimming in the stream of lively conversation!

12. *Other methods* might include sociometry, photography, clinical supervision, highly structured observation by an outsider, checklists, coding scales and much more. The best methods often arise when you are frustrated in using someone else's methods and you invent your own. Just be sure to clearly articulate what you are doing, and keep accurate records of both the content and the permissions you obtained. For example, after writing the chapter on master's projects, Alison Henry wrote to all those students,

now alum authors, to ask for permission. She shared the proposed text with them and now we both have a file with their explicit, written permissions.

Educational research should include a literature review. What has been published on your theme? My students at Antioch have historically used an ERIC search, but thanks to ever expanding internet sources, there are many possibilities. Rather than a scarcity of material, the danger these days has more to do with information overload. Even if one only scans some of the material, it is good to know what others have done and the sources available on a selected theme/question.

Finally, I need to say a few words about "human subjects testing" (more on ethics of research later in this publication). Each professional field has its own guidelines, and it is *essential* that researchers follow these guidelines. Any intervention that can affect the subjects being investigated must be scrutinized from this perspective. For instance, when I did my case studies, I asked the teachers involved to sign a consent form. Among other things, I promised not to release the information gathered to employers, to omit names if quotes are used, and in general, to do everything possible to respect the rights of those participating. In school situations, one may have to obtain parental consent for certain kinds of research. It is best to consult these professional guidelines *ahead of time*. At Antioch we use APA7 guidelines, which contains a consent form. All doing research are asked to get APA7, even if it is a used copy (see https://apastyle.apa.org).

For those who want to read a much more comprehensive study of qualitative research, I suggest *Qualitative Evaluation and Research Methods* by Michael Quinn Patton. One can also consult teacher journals and go online to read about research conferences and presentations.

9

Qualitative Research Design: The Five Essential Components

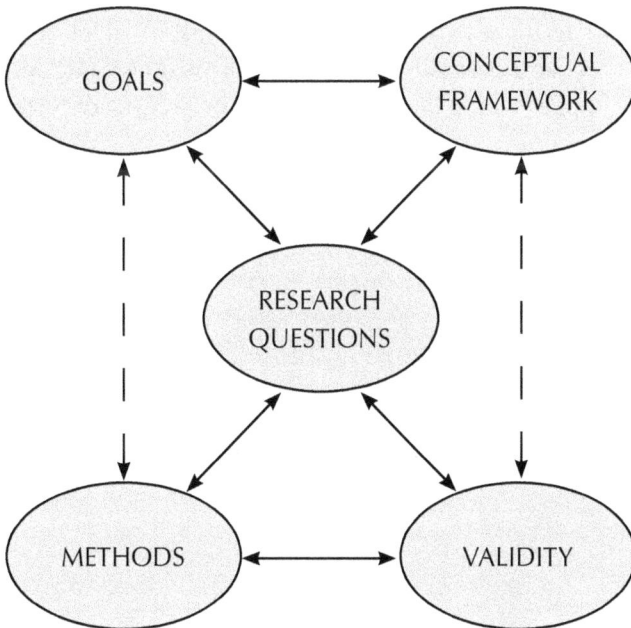

After Joseph A. Maxwell, Qualitative Research Design: An Interactive Approach, *2nd ed., SAGE, 2004*[24]

1. ***Goals.*** Why is your study worth doing? Why do you want to conduct this study, and why should we care about the results?
2. ***Conceptual Framework.*** What do you think is going on with the issues, settings, or people you plan to study? What theories, beliefs, and prior research findings

or personal experiences will guide or inform your
research?

3. **Research Questions.** What, *specifically*, do you want to
understand by doing this study? What do we *not* know
about the phenomenon under consideration? What
questions will your research attempt to answer, and
how are they related to one another?

4. **Methods.** What will you actually do in this study? What
methods will you use to collect and analyze your data?

5. **Validity.** How can you ensure that the data you collect
a) addresses your research questions, b) yields correct and defensible answers to those questions, and c)
applies to the larger population or process of interest?

10

Organizing a Research Project

Picture yourself being outrageously successful in all the work discussed so far. Now you have a burning question, lots of material has been collected through the use of documents, interviews, observations, case studies, and so on, and everything is heaped up on a special shelf at home, a designated file(s) on your computer—all in one or two happy jumbles. There are many, when faced with this spectacle, who abandon the whole process at this point. Indeed, for the natural "pack rats" in our midst, it is far easier to amass a literary fortune than to organize, let alone analyze, the material. Yet, it is essential for the research process that one goes beyond collection to comprehension. Organizing the material involves considered synthesis before one can start on analysis.

I suggest you begin by outlining some broad categories within your theme. Separate your material accordingly. You may well change your categories after a while, but in the initial sorting you are also beginning to "mix and match" information that will create new insights. Be sure to go through all the data. An outline should actually have been done much earlier in the process, but now is the ultimate end date—it is impossible to organize without clarity of topics, sequence etc.

Now you arrive at the weeding phase. Harry Wolcott describes this well:

The critical task in qualitative research is not to accumulate all the data you can, but to "can" (i.e., get rid of) most of the data you accumulate. This requires constant winnowing. The trick is to discover essences and then to reveal them within sufficient context, without being mired by trying to include everything that could be described. Audio tapes, videotapes, and now computer capabilities entreat us to do just the opposite; they have gargantuan appetites and stomachs. Because we can accommodate ever-increasing quantities of data—mountains of it—we have to be careful not to get buried by avalanches of our own making.[25]

In organizing, as with preparation for teaching, it is not how much material you have, but rather how well you have worked it through. This sifting and sorting help to connect you with the essentials.

A few practical suggestions:

1. Use separate index cards and/or separate computer files, with the title of a category at the top of each section. You can move the cards or files around as need arises, but having the headings in front of you will keep things organized. In doing this new version of my research pamphlet, I actually took all the files for the separate chapters and lined them up on a row on my desktop. One can then move them around depending on new insights.

2. In terms of facts, figures and especially citations, get them right the first time. As I found when editing *School as a Journey*, one inaccurate or missing page number in the footnotes can take hours to rectify. Keep accurate records. One added challenge: SteinerBooks and other publishers often come out with a new version of a book, new title, introduction etc., yet you may have read an earlier version. Generally, in scholarship, we

are encouraged to use the latest edition, but that can be a time consuming (and at times expensive) chore. But make sure the source you cite in the footnotes is the same edition as in the bibliography!

3. If you are going to write up your findings, decide early on if you will use the *Chicago Manual of Style* for your field or the APA standards. This can save a lot of time later on. At Antioch, we just tell all our students to use APA7 (see https://apastyle.apa.org).

4. Keep a pencil and small notebook on you at all times. Even after the formal gathering of data is over (actually, it is never over, you just have to decide when to stop), you can have sudden inspirations or ideas that need to be noted down. Take advantage of the higher levels of cognition described in the last chapter—they are the gifts of the gods. Even long meetings are remarkably productive in birthing inspirational thoughts. Keep your notebook by your side.

As you are sorting things out, it helps to know what your general intent might be:

Are you doing basic research in a general way so as to contribute to the fundamental knowledge available on a given subject?

Are you doing *applied research* to illuminate a societal concern?

Or might you engage in *summative evaluation* to determine the effectiveness of a particular program?

On the other hand, you might intend to perform a *formative evaluation* to actually help improve a program.

Are you doing *action research* to solve a specific problem?[26]

Intentions give shape and form to material one gathers and organizes.

Then, when one has a good handle on *what* is available and *why* one is doing this work, it is time to start the analysis of the data. I find, at least in the student research that I review, that this aspect is usually the weakest, partly because it is given the least time, and partly because real analysis is strenuous and challenging. Most people are good at summarizing, but that is not analysis. Over the years I have had to be much more specific in coaching research projects by asking questions that provoke analysis: How do these findings compare with other studies? Are there contradictions between your work and that of others? How can you relate one subtopic in your project to another? What happens when you combine the results of your survey with the interview transcripts? How does this research relate to your own experience? How do things interact with one another in your mind, and how do the perceptions of school values and beliefs interact with student learning?

One can move things around, draw diagrams, look at things from a variety of perspectives, and in the process, real analysis can begin.

Collecting material is like going shopping, which is easy for most people. Organizing challenges some, and synthesizing the material is more challenging, much like preparing a meal. But the most complicated process of all, if one really stops to consider it, is the eating/digesting of the food. Research without analysis is like swallowing food without chewing properly. Good research values all stages of the process, including the nourishment and sharing that occurs when the food of learning is put to use (see playful spoof on cooking in appendix). A former student wrote:

> I had no idea how much I was to learn doing this research!
> What began as an idea to incorporate the travel experience

(somehow) into the learning environment of the Waldorf high school student eventually turned into a study of [evil] forces at work in ancient Mayan ritual! And I got to bring twelve Waldorf high school students to the ancient sites in the Yucatan (for a two-week trip) to boot! You never know where [the process of] research will lead you. A *tiny idea* can turn into a *career*. We ask questions that only we could ask. We investigate because it has become so much a part of what we find we need to know.

In our teaching, we can take what we've learned, of course, and apply it in the classroom. But just as important—through our striving to understand our subject (via research)—we naturally reflect this striving to our children, giving them a quiet example to which they can aspire.

11

Ethical Considerations in Research

In August 1919, a few weeks before giving the first set of training lectures to future Waldorf teachers, Rudolf Steiner mentioned in *Education as a Social Problem* a few of the challenges of our time. One is still with us today: egoism.

In research, we need to look at our motivation and intentions. "The habit of valuing everything only in reference to one's personal interest" (common definition of egoism) can be an issue in starting a project, seeking an MEd or PhD. Some simply want to advance in terms of professional development and career goals. There is nothing wrong with that. But when self-interest or conceit flows into actual research and interaction with sources, colleagues and friends, problems can arise. Exploitation can be a danger in research just as with the environment, indigenous traditions, cultural appropriation or plagiarism.

When we do research, do we seek to learn just for ourselves or in order to better serve? What do I plan to do with my new insights? What will the impact be on those I study? How will it affect my school, colleagues, parents and the wider community? These and other questions need to be asked to "clear our lenses" *and know not just what but how and why we are doing research.*

Building on the work of Jo-ann Archibald (in *Decolonizing Research;* see next section), we might place four key words before out soul, words that speak volumes in terms of our intentions, methods and ethical conduct:

Respect

Responsibility

Reverence

Reciprocity

There is so much that can be said about each of the above, but I urge my readers to dwell on them for a while. What do respect, responsibility, reverence, and reciprocity mean to you? When have you experienced these attributes and when have you seen humans fall short? Not just in the indigenous context, but in the treatment of all human beings? How can we become "story-ready" or what I might call "research-ready"?

A lot of this self-examination has to do with considering the impact of our work ahead of time. Who will I engage in my process, when and how, and what steps can I take to create safe spaces for my interviews and other interactions? In some situations, we need to do more than consider these four key words but also do a CITI training in human subjects testing and get approval from an internal review board housed in a university. In many cases, one needs to work with an advisor who can help guide ethical practices. But in all the situations I have known, the inner path and growing self-awareness is foundational for ethical practices in research. Therefore, in our Antioch Waldorf Program research courses we couple the theme of research with the study of anthroposophy as a method of inquiry. Personal and professional growth need to journey together.

12

Learning from Indigenous Ways

In the introduction to *Decolonizing Research, Indigenous Storywork as Methodology* (Bloomsbury Academic 2019), Jo-ann Archibald (Q'um Q'um Xiiem) names the four previously mentioned principles of **respect, responsibility, reverence and reciprocity** as an ethical guide for researchers working with Indigenous people, their knowledge and stories.

These four principles must stand for all those doing research today and should certainly guide Waldorf teachers in their work. This involves so many facets of research, from working with sources, to interviews, observations etc. Using holistic approaches has been a core tenet of Waldorf from the beginning.

Some think of colonization mainly in a sociopolitical and historical context. But some of the same dynamics can be found when the powerful "elite" exercise colonizing influences in academia. Who designed some of the "Western" approaches to research, (not to mention standardized tests)? What are the accepted practices that many take up without questioning? "Colonial Western research of our traditional stories and research stories of our peoples was used to define, destroy, and deter the valuing of Indigenous knowledge, people, and practices" (p. 5).

Behind the "façade" of objectivity, much research has taken a position of racial superiority and has misrepresented, misappropriated and misused Indigenous stories. Jo-ann Archibald goes on to say that this is more than "theft" of cultural property, it is "an intellectual, cultural, and spiritual invasion" (p. 5).

For the readers who cannot devote the time to the complete book cited here, I would like to lift a few key concepts especially from Jo-ann's article to highlight considerations for teachers doing research in their teacher education programs:

1. "The relationship of the researcher to their community is central to understanding one as Indigenous" (p. 7).

When we designed a course at Antioch called Education for Social Renewal many years ago (1994), we built in a strong community component. This included the group work on sharing initial questions, using research methods in schools that were not only CITI compliant but also deeply respectful of those we engage in the projects. From the beginning we used journal partners to provide professional and emotional support as well as make sure we are seen and recognized. The addition of group zoom sessions in recent years has helped, such as problem-solving sessions when everyone contributes (and not just the instructor). But most of all, we celebrate achievement and share research projects with a live audience when students return after twelve months. They present and then meet in small groups with the audience for feedback and conversation. (See contribution from Debbie Spitulnik below.) In short, the whole research process at Antioch is designed to accentuate the importance of community. If one experiences community as a cohort, one is more likely to strive for the same in schools as professional learning communities.

2. "In Aotearoa (New Zealand), *purakau* was one Māori narrative form" (p. 89).

It is especially important for teachers to find their voice. To do so, they need to learn to tell stories! Learning the stories from cultures all over the world affords a splendid opportunity not only to create a diverse curriculum, but also to learn to hear the "voice" of the story in a variety of ways. We need to tell stories from our own lives and learn to appreciate those of others.

Research involves a narrative. Rather than just a summary of collected sources and citations, good research does analysis and carries themes that are transparent and helpful. Some of my students are great at treasure hunting and come up with pages of material they have collected. Others are better at weaving and thinking between the sources, doing analysis. We need both. Generally, I have struggled more with encouraging true analysis (as well as keeping distinction between synthesis and analysis in student papers). This should not be surprising, since our world today is packed with information but often affords little time for reflection.

When successful, a teacher learns to use research as an opportunity to go deep, find residual questions and work with them over time. We need reflective practitioners who are able to give intentional guidance and meaning to their work in the classroom.

3. Joeliee Seed-Pihama describes the way in which *korero ingoa* (naming stories) work to reassert and reclaim Māori names and culture. Stories can "speak back" and "speak forward" not only to help understand but also to transform.[27]

A name is closely connected to identity, and naming stories can be crucial in advocacy. The research projects teachers-in- training do are often connected with a quest to find oneself. That is why it is so important that we spend enough time on selecting a question or theme in the first place. It needs to surface from the deep recesses of consciousness to have the transformative power we seek. A good project works toward clarification of identity, purpose, meaning and finding Self. With this effort, we can all become better advocates for the social and pedagogical changes we seek.

4. "Researchers in these [Indigenous] communities must guard against the imposition of methods of collecting, analyzing, and reporting 'fact' in ways that are not culturally sensitive and that fail to safeguard the lives of the people they study" (p. 154). This statement speaks for itself; thus, my only addition is that teachers need to extend this imperative to their work with any children they involve in their research projects. Parental permissions, CITI training (human subjects), APA7 guidelines and other precautions need to be observed to protect and cherish those who are vulnerable.

5. Trees: Jenny Bol Jun Lee-Morgan: "In Aotearoa [New Zealand], our young trees do not have tap roots, because the older and more established trees provide support to the young ones. Without taproots, the young trees literally depend on each other to grow" (p. 155). "The diversity of stories from various perspectives provide a richer, fuller, more colorful, and probably more lifelike portrait" (p. 156). "Multiple and different interpretations can be valuable simultaneously" (p. 157).

How can we enhance the interconnections through research? The image of the forest is beautiful. When individuals in a group engage in research simultaneously, they form a web just as in a New Zealand forest. This provides a vibrant source of nourishment for the individuals as well as for the schools they represent.

The preceding quotation poses a challenge particularly in this time we live in: can we allow multiple and different perspectives (and interpretations) to live side by side simultaneously? It is not easy!

We are easily drawn to our own preferences, affinity groups and areas of comfort. Many want things to fit neatly into place. I often hear the thought: "I am not comfortable with..." Some see the world in stark polarities: us and them. The notion that there may be *several perspectives* is not easy to process.

Research gives us an opportunity to respectfully entertain more than the usual simplistic views on a given matter. And thanks to the sources I have been working with, we can *all learn* to see through the eyes of Indigenous cultures that were able to see and appreciate the diversity of stories and the multiple interpretations of them.

Finally, there is working from the core of the tree:

Ruia taitea, kia tu ko taikaka anake—Cast aside the sapwood, and let the heartwood alone stand (Mead and groves, 2003, p. 351 quoted in *Decolonizing Research*, p. 161).

What is the core of our research subject? Despite the flowers or apples on our "tree," how can we go *inside to the core and find the essence?* In my own research it is sometimes like a maze, one circles in and in, not always knowing where one is going. Yet there is a general sense of direction. And it is so important, ever so important, that one keeps moving!

Sometimes I feel lost, can't tell left from right, but the movement has its own genius, and gradually my thoughts learn to follow my feet. Just do it, I keep saying.

Then after some time one has discovery moments: So, this is what I am *really researching*! Over time (and time is so important), one finds a way to the core. And when one arrives at the core issues of a topic, one knows it. Eureka. There is no mistaking the core of the tree or of a topic. Then one can start to spiral out again, renewed with new certainty and confidence. Along the way back out there are new things to gather, sources and resources, and one emerges back on the outside with a paper, talk or new learning for life. This is the tree of research and of life. It can speak a truth.

13

Sharing Research

If the kind of action research described in the foregoing pages is to have legitimacy within the larger circles of our profession, it needs to be shared. This not only means the articulation of what we have discovered, but the feedback and consequent corrective measures that are needed.

Although we may never feel we know enough on a given subject to share the results of our research, we do know something, and even that needs the enhancement of feedback. Sharing puts one in a vulnerable position; there are risks involved. Yet the social and intellectual benefits are great. One basic way to begin is to write.

In a marvelous article that appears in *Handbook of Qualitative Research*, Laurel Richardson states, "I consider writing as a method of inquiry, a way of finding out about yourself and your topic.... Writing is also a way of "knowing"—a method of discovery and analysis. By writing in different ways, we discover new aspects of our topic and our relationship to it."[28] Thus, writing is continued research, only on a different level. You are able to enter the imaginative realm as you become the creator of images.

I suggest you begin with a one-paragraph statement of purpose. If you cannot say the gist of your piece in one terse paragraph, it will certainly be harder to write a book. A statement of purpose can be as simple as the articulation of the issue or question studied, why you took it up, and the results. Remember in this whole endeavor, you are not trying to prove or define anything. Just describe and characterize and you will bring people along with you.

A characterization looks at things from several angles, keeps the image alive, focuses on the qualities, and does not try and define. Sometimes I advise students to pick up the phone and call a good friend. When the inevitable question arises, "So, what have you been doing lately," just turn on a tape recorder and say something about your research, why you took it up and the bottom line—the findings. Then after the rest of the phone conversation is over, replay the section on your research and write it down. It will need some editing, but most likely you have the gist of a statement of purpose.

My emphasis on this first stage comes from experience in reading student research reports and masters-level projects. If the first part, the purpose, is not in focus, everything else becomes much more difficult. There is a special kind of "soul economy" in spending the time chiseling a clear statement describing what the project is all about.

Then it is a natural next step to do an outline or sequence. Again, if past experiences with this sort of thing are intimidating, think of it as a table of contents. What are the main topics? In what order should they appear? Think about ways in which you can connect people with your work. What would interest your colleagues, your students' parents?

A solid outline can mark the start of some serious writing. However, in my experience, things have never been as linear as they seem on this page. I have found myself writing snippets even as the research progressed, and therefore the actual outline changes as one releases the creative stream of the narrative. The basic elements described here are important, but the actual experience, at least for me, is of unexpected simultaneity.

Along with "math phobia," "writer's block" ranks high on many people's most dreaded list. In large part, this is because writing is placed on such a high pedestal. It seems that many people subconsciously feel that if their work is not a best-seller they have failed as writers. Here you need to remember the previously cited words from Laurel Richardson. If writing is part of the process of discovery, you might lower your sights, practice some humility, and just aim to understand the material collected in a new way. Start the writing as a *reflection* on your findings. Begin in a conversational manner, just talking about your research. Use the pen or computer to do the talking. Don't worry about paragraphs or anything remotely close to proper grammar. Just say something about your work.

Harry Wolcott adds, "Writing is a form of thinking. Writers who indulge themselves by waiting until their thoughts are 'clear' run the risk of never starting at all."[29] Put something down on your screen or paper. If you are using word processing, it is easy to make deletions, cut and paste, and correct mistakes. Before the computer, doctoral candidates took twice as long to complete their studies.

In addition to technical assistance, the process of writing is enhanced by a certain amount of self-knowledge. Are you a morning or evening person? Do you need a stiff cup of coffee to get going, or a brisk walk? Know what works for you, and then use it. For me, the early morning is writing time. Beginning in early May, I used to rise early each day and do one narrative, class-teacher report each morning. After

school was out, it was just a matter of editing and copying—
a sufficiently onerous project in those warm June days. But
my summer vacations often began earlier than others.

Another suggestion: Consider the point at which you will
quit each session and how to take up the writing again later.
Instead of stopping at the end of a topic or section, I often find
it best to stop just before the logical resting place or end of a
chapter. This means that, at the next session, I was forced to
reread the previous section, do some editing, and then jump
back into the stream of things without having to pull everything up from scratch. Again, the important thing is knowing
what works for you.

Another statement of the obvious: the shorter the piece,
the more likely the possibility it will find readers. Qualitative
research is meant to be read and used. If you can say it in a
few words, do so.

Finally, at some point in the write-up you will need to
inform the readers about the nature and extent of your data-
base, how you collected the material and the methods used.
They need to know how you went about your work, since
the process influences the results. Again, when I read student
papers, I usually turn first to the annotated bibliography.
That tells me about process and enlightens my reading of the
full text.

These teacher research projects can be used for presentation in staff meetings, at a school board discussion of a particular topic, or as a brief piece in a local newspaper. Teachers
can hold mini conferences to share their work, and schools
could list completed projects in newsletters that go to parents.
We need to be willing to make our work in education more
visible. Remember—*silence is complicity.*

In 1992, the Waldorf Teacher Education Program at Antioch New England launched a summer sequence program for experienced educators. From the beginning, research was an integral part of the first year, as the students selected a theme to work with between the first and second summer sessions. After a year of "living with a question" and doing research as described in this book, they returned the following summer to take further courses and share their findings. I asked them to share reflections on the research process, some of which are included here and throughout this book.

The research and deepening of one's work, in my case foreign language teaching, can ignite renewed forces from within which can manifest themselves as enthusiasm and interest in one's teaching and working with the children. Through a deeper esoteric understanding and research in one's field and as an anthroposophist, the knowledge gained through research brings one closer together with fellow Waldorf teachers in a common striving. In this way, we can support each other and nurture each other through sharing of our work and findings. (Sandra Houston)

Researching my topic was an opportunity to step back and understand the context the Waldorf schools occupy with regards to public education. By characterizing the public school approach to environmental education and science, I was able to go on to survey just what had been founded as an approach to nature in the Waldorf Schools. The most important aspect of the research was the new insights, which I was able to synthesize and develop from the wide range of literature, which I surveyed. My ability to speak intelligently about the Waldorf approach has greatly improved, and I believe my opinions are authentically grounded now in my own efforts and understanding. I would recommend research as a discipline to anyone who would wish to usher Waldorf *education into the next century.* (Gregory Albright)

My anthroposophical research has a threefold quality to it: the reading, the writing and the presentation. I found the quiet inner activity of research complemented the busy outer activity of my days. Reading with a question, a focus, increased my depth and encouraged me to wrestle with the material. This had a vivifying effect on my life. The process of writing went beyond compilation: it was as if all that I had taken in nurtured a seed within me. In tending this seed, it gradually ripened until something new had grown in me. Writing out of this inner conclusion was exhilarating. I then entered the social realm with the presentation of the essence of my work. This inspired me to take my paper to a different level, an imaginative "audience friendly" one, which led me to new insights on my topic. I breathed in with the research and out with the presentation. The whole process greatly strengthened me physically, emotionally and mentally. I have a solid footing in one aspect of Anthroposophy now and a matrix to which I can relate new information and insights. The spiral continues. The fruits multiply. (Kathleen Reagan)

Winter evenings reading and carrying images into sleep; trips to the library, telephone conversations, stints at the computer—beginning to write things down. Searching, looking and finding again. Research? Gathering scattered threads together, starting to weave. Just a small piece of cloth, but so satisfying! Fit one small piece to another small piece, the cloth grows. This work made a rich and private inner haven for me—the task of writing, bringing my thoughts and feelings to form; seeing the rich colors swirl into shape and solidify. This was both a discovery and an exercise of will. Finally, presenting my winter-work to a group of colleagues spread the whole cloth out, a blanket for our mental picnic. I experienced this task as a way of connecting—with myself, with others and with the world that holds us all. (Kate Gage)

Research Presentations: Reflections from Debbie Spitulnik, Long-time Antioch Adjunct

As the students filled my classroom, the buzz was louder than usual. This was a speech class, so always a place filled with sounds, but today was different. It was the day of the group's research presentations. They were excited, nervous and brave. Studies have shown that public speaking ranks among the top fears people face. The Antioch students are fortunate enough to have the opportunity, and the training, to overcome this fear. Through the research of a topic that touches their heart and curiosity and is relevant to their lives, they build a presentation that will speak to the hearts and minds of their audience.

I have attended these presentations of research projects for years. Each time I am impressed with the student, the topic, the presentation itself, and the format and form of the event. These graduate students have been given the scaffolding of both the activity of researching a topic, and of bringing it together as an interesting, inspiring and artistic presentation. I am fascinated and impressed at the topics that are presented. Many of them I had not thought deeply about, or had wondered about but not been able to do the research myself. This format gives those of us in the audience the ability to grow in our understanding of education and Anthroposophy and learn as community.

After everyone has presented, Torin Finser gathers his thoughts and makes comments about each presentation, weaving them all together in a coherent way that makes sense as a whole. Then we as an audience have the opportunity to speak with each presenter in small groups, give our impressions, ask questions and give well deserved congratulations.

This form of a research project and presentation often changes the course of a student's life and career. It certainly did for me. My project in researching Creative Speech and the Development of Consciousness has become my vocation, my life's work. As is the case with many students, I had never spoken in front of a large group of people before our Antioch presentations.

The opportunity to learn more about a topic and oneself is enhanced by finding the essence of research, creating a presentation that is articulate, artistic and interesting, and then breathing life into it through the spoken word. Fear of public speaking is replaced by growth and exhilaration. When it all comes together it is magic.

14

A Sampling of Recent Master's Projects: Advocacy through Research

by Alison Henry, PhD

Each year, students in Antioch University New England's Waldorf programs[30] who seek to earn their master's degree in education undertake deeply meaningful research, not only contributing to their own personal and professional development but also enriching Waldorf and anthroposophical communities with their findings. Students have conducted highly relevant action research, insightful case studies, philosophical and spiritual explorations, and practical survey research. Whether they opt to write a traditional academic thesis or undertake a capstone project of their own design, these students continually impress us with what they offer to our community.

In fall 2023, Will Minehart III completed his master's project on the connections between spirituality, ecological identity work, and Waldorf education. To explore this sacred connection, Will combined elements of both a thesis and capstone approach, including detailed surveys, in-depth interviews, observations from his own teaching practice, and a workshop with colleagues. In a richly worded final paper Will was able to share a broad set of findings with implications for how teachers can cultivate their students' deep connection to the natural world. Among the many highlights of Will's final thesis is a literature review in which Will highlights the overlap between what is called *ecospirituality* in the realm of environmental education, on the one hand, and Rudolf Steiner's insights into the connection between building a relationship to the natural world and building a relationship to the spiritual world, on the other. Teachers will find inspiration here for their own personal development and for the enrichment of their teaching practice inside and outside the classroom.

In fall 2021, **Kimberly Sinclair** completed her master's project on extended, after-school care from an anthroposophical perspective. Building on her own experience designing and implementing a nourishing after-school program for her school, Kimberly used her master's project as an opportunity to gather insights from other Waldorf schools who provide after-school care or vacation camps, as well as interview leaders in the Waldorf movement about both the history of extended care in Waldorf schools and the indications and recommendations for making extended care as nourishing as possible for children. School leaders and teachers will find a wealth of information here about trends in after-school care provided by Waldorf schools, as well as insights for working with temperaments, transitions, and mixed-aged groups, among many considerations. Kimberly's final thesis includes rich anecdotes and concrete examples of the many challenges faced by after-school care providers, but it also discusses specific ways to address those same challenges.

In fall 2020, **Andrew May** completed his master's project on the collaboration between teachers and an anthroposophical school doctor in a Waldorf school. Even before he began this project, Andrew had been exploring the connection between a child's cognitive development and observations about the child's constitution, for example, made by the school doctor. Andrew's master's project, then, gave him the opportunity to fully explore the important transdisciplinary relationship between the physiological aspects of child development that are inseparable from the child's cognitive and psychological development. Andrew's thesis will be of particular interest to practitioners who seek insight into the special collaboration that Steiner foresaw between teachers and a school doctor. One of the many highlights of Andrew's final thesis is the way in which he moves beyond any simple notion of a literature review and, instead, engages the literature on this pedagogical-medical connection in a rich textual analysis that yields fascinating connections and deep insights.

In fall 2022, **Thea Bieling** completed her master's project, in which she explored how shame operates in schools and classrooms and can lead to enduring harm for all those affected. Thea began her research with an analysis of closely related terminology, highlighting various definitions, including embodied, somatic descriptions of shame. Thea also considered the individualistic and sociocultural experience of shame through the theoretical lens of power and oppression, with particular attention to the perspective brought by the Radical Therapy Collective. Thea's final paper includes the voices of her participants sharing their lived experience of shame, and their active efforts to identify ways in which shame and shaming can infiltrate the classroom. In the end, Thea finds promise in the practice of building *shame-resilience*, which allows one to respond to shame with context, vulnerability, and self-compassion instead of what Thea identifies as immobilizing or aggressive behaviors. Teachers who have not considered how shame may be present in their classrooms will find a helpful guide in this master's project.

In spring 2022, **Rochelle Dietz** completed her master's project based on a community care workshop she designed and implemented. In another excellent example of the capstone option, Rochelle researched and designed a full day workshop in which her participants enjoyed an engaging set of activities around three key themes: levity, laughter, and love. During the workshop, Rochelle led participants in activities as diverse as free dance, skits, and quiet one-on-one activities, and at various points during the workshop, participants had the opportunity to pause, reflect, and share their experiences on brief survey questionnaires, which Rochelle collected for her own process of reflection and learning. Rochelle's final paper provides a glimpse of the rich, healing experience she created, but, as with any capstone, the final paper was secondary to the nourishing experience she created in the workshop itself.

In summer 2023, **Angelique Metta** completed her master's project on innovation and adaptation to ensure that Waldorf curriculum is place-based and responsive to the needs of children now and in the future. Drawing on her own extensive experience in grass-roots community development, Angelique set out to address, if not eliminate, the barriers that have stifled innovation in Waldorf classrooms, building a compelling argument that Waldorf education was always designed to be place-based and culturally responsive. To complement her extensive literature review and theoretical framework, Angelique conducted interviews with leaders of self-identified innovative Waldorf schools from around the world, gathering insights about how they have transformed the traditional Waldorf curriculum for their own students and community while remaining true to the fundamental vision of Waldorf education. Teachers and school leaders may be interested in the *Waldorf Conscious Change Manual* that Angelique curated based on a variety of resources and her own personal experiences, designed to help schools undertake a process of self-exploration toward innovation. This is one of the many useful resources that Angelique included in her appendices.

In fall 2023, **Tess Hamilton** completed her master's project on intergenerational living and learning communities. In particular, Tess sought to explore how elder care and early childhood education could be re-imagined in an intentional community setting, with the entire community benefitting from this more holistic model of education and living. Tess's interview findings, alone, will be revelatory for those unfamiliar with intentional communities. Readers of Tess's final paper will note that Tess draws upon her own experiences growing up in an intentional community, as well as the insights she gleaned as a Watson fellow, when she traveled for a year and lived in thirteen distinct communities around the world to look at the *social ecology of home*. In many respects, this master's project is a natural extension of her Watson fellowship, as Tess brings the wisdom and insights of those communities back with her and imagines how she can help transform the individualistic, consumer-based community models that abound in this country. While Tess's project has elements of both a capstone and a thesis, her final paper is an excellent resource for anyone interested in creating or supporting an intentional, intergenerational learning community.

The projects featured here are but a small sampling of the many projects that our students have completed over the years. In each case, the final product, whether a thesis or capstone, usually represents the culmination of more than a year of focused study, research, engagement and writing. While students experience inevitable challenges and frustrations along the way, student after student has shared that the process is truly transformative. Even for those students who start their master's project with a clear idea of where they think they will end up, the journey is filled with opportunities for revelation and self-discovery. We, the faculty, could not be prouder. As a faculty and program committed to nurturing and renewing Waldorf education and anthroposophy in the world, we sense in each project a unique gift, a fresh insight into how we, individually and collectively, can best meet the highest ideals of Waldorf education and anthroposophically guided practice in our communities.

15

A Collaborative Model for Teacher Research
Building a Culture of Research in a School

Looking at the larger picture of teacher stress and renewal, as I did during my doctoral research, I found that caregivers—nurses, parents, and teachers—also need nurturing. To give without replenishment is to limit one's capacity to continue. How can one find the resources for personal and professional renewal?

I found that many teachers, despite participating in numerous meetings, often felt a high degree of isolation. Not only do our tasks limit the time we can converse together on a personal level, but the level of expectations is such that many feel inadequate, whether it be in drawing, singing, math or speech. It is hard to reach out from a position of vulnerability and ask for support. Often, just as one is about to, a crisis comes along, and we go back to the "day-to-day" survival mentality, and the armor of invincibility goes back on. How can we better share our striving as human beings?

Collaborative research is an attempt to address these and other school issues. Collaboration means to work together, doing what any single one of us could not do alone. If one really means this then collaboration is not just a matter of sharing "results," but must characterize *each stage* of the research process. How can one be realistic, given the limitations of time and resources (see first section) and yet do research together? Is it possible to envision a model that is simple and yet multifaceted, one that does not take too much organizing and yet addresses other social and spiritual issues in the lives of teachers?

One clue comes from the traditions of oral history. Describing a collective project of residents of Hackney in East London, Thompson (1978) reports the interviews of community members and their lives with the intent of giving "back to people their own history, on the one hand, to build up through a series of individual accounts a composite history of life and work in Hackney, and, on the other, to give people confidence in their own memories of the past, their ability to contribute to the writing of history—confidence in their own words: in short, in themselves."[30] In olden times, people would sit around the fireplace on a cold winter evening and tell stories—tales that would be passed down from one generation to the other. There was a thread of continuity here, and the group or family found its identity reflected in the oral traditions. The "bard" or storyteller of olden times has been replaced in most modern living rooms with flat panel TVs that do not serve the same purpose. We need to recreate cultural traditions and rituals more consciously if we are to hold on to our humanity. Researching and retelling what one has found is one way to reawaken human connections.

The previously mentioned project involving the creation of an oral history reminded me that adults learn best from each other and through sharing experiences. This awareness has helped me formulate the following model for collaborative research:

A. Hearing Our Questions in Our Schools

I suggest that when back at school in the fall, faculty share their questions as described earlier in this text. One might begin by asking that each teacher take ten minutes to quietly write down her/his "wonderings." Then divide the faculty into groups of three to share. The two members of each group that are listening would see themselves as coaches, first asking their colleague what kind of feedback would help, then perhaps asking questions for clarification, helping find connections between the wonderings, and in general, encourage. The roles in the small groups would then switch. At the end of the small-group sessions, each teacher should affirm the feedback received and choose one question that is of greatest importance. This coaching stage needs at least an hour. Then the faculty could reconvene, and the chair could set the tone with a few words about their "circle of trust" and the spirit in which questions are shared. This might make it possible for each teacher to share a question that could serve as a companion for the school year, a question that has enough passion to enthuse commitment.

Example question: How can teachers best meet the learning and developmental needs of boys?

B. Finding a Structure for Questions

Much time can be saved if the research process is looked at from the viewpoint of methodology at this early point. I suggest that we look to the education departments of interested universities to provide research consultants to visit the schools that have undertaken this project and meet with colleagues individually to draw up an outline of how, when and where the research will be conducted. Some things could be demonstrated in a large group setting such as the faculty meeting, but other issues are really based on individual situations, and the methods used in research must suit the particular question. By having, say, the same consultant visits several schools, he or she could help teachers from different schools connect, based on shared interests. This "research web" would gradually provide a new layer of "association."

Example: Pose the question about boys at a faculty meeting, a teachers' conference or a family gathering, and ask participants to voluntarily fill out a questionnaire that you will leave on the table. Be willing to do this for other people's projects.

C. Following a Question

This stage involves data collection, as described above. I suggest that the faculty again find small groups to serve as a monthly "check-in," at which time each member would expect to hear an update on the progress. The importance here is not approval or even feedback, but rather staying with the task and reporting on progress. Support listening is crucial. This process is very much part of learning. As stated by Jon Wagner, "Research itself is a form of learning, and research reporting a form of teaching."[31]

Example: Do diary entries on your classroom observations of boys and how they respond in different classes.

D. Collegial Review

About halfway through the year, each teacher could write a brief three-to-five-page narrative, describing the project— a sort of overview. This narrative would be shared in the cohort group of three and sent to the research consultant for review. This collegial review, if handled rightly, can be tremendously affirming, lessen the stress issues around research, and enhance the social life within a school through shared interests. The responses from peers could be gathered and used as an assessment tool.

Example: Present some preliminary findings on the question of boys' development at a gathering of peers and ask for feedback. The responses will inform you about how you are communicating and what resonates with other teachers.

E. The Symposium

I envision that in the spring there could be a festive symposium, in which three to four schools could hold a weekend conference to share some of their research projects. I suggest that the host school not be one that has done the collaborative research, so that the presenters are free to focus on their sharing. Each school should send the topics proposed for the conference to the research consultant, who would group them thematically. Also, some teachers might need to be dissuaded or encouraged. The consultant could also serve as the convener at the weekend conference, setting the tone for presentations to follow. Proceedings could occasionally be published, thus helping to change the often-one-sided focus of the media on testing and outcome-based assessment.

Example: Present a more formal "paper" on how teachers today are meeting the needs of boys. Distribute evaluation forms afterward. Use them as part of your analysis.

I suggest that each presentation be no more than twenty to thirty minutes, the distilled essence of a year's work. The inner activity in this process of winnowing can be rewarding for the presenter and helps keep the audience focused. One might have three to four such presentations around a common theme, preceded by speech or singing. After each cluster, I suggest a short break and then discussion groups that would look at themes arising from the reports and provide a vehicle for questions to the presenters, and thus the recapitulation of the entire process that began with questions. One might have one group of presentations on Friday evening, one each on Saturday morning, Saturday afternoon and Sunday morning. The conference could end with a plenum of "the research process," thus allowing for the rewrite of this book.

This symposium format, with the feedback mechanism built into the structure, also allows for a response to the Heisenberg Effect—the uncertainty principle—which might cause some to question the accuracy of any study, since the observer/researcher may have affected the results by simply being a part of the equation.[32] One of the best ways to check up on ourselves and our biases is to share the results with the informants (those who participated) and our colleagues. Teachers know when something rings true or needs modification. Our colleagues are our best recourse in dealing with the uncertainty principle.

Please note what is not included in the above: antiseptic methods, a long research paper, onerous deadlines, and lots of extracurricular activities. Teachers already do much of what has been described. They go to conferences, read, meet, share, and so on. Simply use the venues already available—just put research sharing on the table for all to partake. This collaborative model is mainly an intensification of teacher preparation, with an eye toward forming a research community.

If possible, the proceedings of the symposium should be recorded as a video (or as a transcript) and edited and then made available to teachers in other regions of North America. Over time, with alternating regions taking this up, a considerable body of primary material would become available to the parents and teachers alike. Even before then, however, the social/transformative benefits would be felt in our schools. Over time, some of the concerns expressed in earlier chapters of this book would be addressed. Teachers would have a greater "voice" in educational decision making, policy might focus more on the real needs of children, and the government might back off when the vitality of the profession is experienced in one community after another. After all, who elects our political leaders anyway? Steven Montgomery from the Waldorf Teacher Education Program at Antioch New England states it thus:

> The activity of research serves two important functions:
> 1) As an exploration in more depth of questions and thoughts which seem important to our individual growth and inner purpose, and 2) as it results in a movement forward to communicate to others what stirs our deepest human interest. This process of articulation is essential to participating actively in the social realm.

16

Research and the Inner Life

The research journey is often deeply connected to personal biography. How did I find my topic/question? Why is this the right one for me at this time in my life? How has my biography influenced my view of the world and myself? If one reflects on these questions over time (see chapter on timeline in research), one often comes to the exciting realization that *my question found me!*

If this is the case, then the mystery of "finding" becomes a prompt to appreciate the research process as more than an academic exercise. It is an opportunity to encounter deep seated themes and questions that may have been carried in the soul for some time already.

Research affords an opportunity to take up the inner work while doing research. For many, a research questions becomes a kind of "companion" that travels with us in the car, airplane, at work, while on a walk—and this companion can open our eyes to both external and internal sources. I urge those who seek self-awareness and fulfillment in life to acknowledge and appreciate this invisible yet helpful companion.

Socrates spoke of the "daemon," in the Middle Ages there was a concept of the personal angel, in other spiritual traditions there has been awareness of the "inner voice," or the bird sitting on the shoulder (Egypt). No matter how it is described and in which culture, one can find ample validation of this notion of the invisible companion that accompanies us through life.

If one accepts this as a real possibility, the next consideration becomes: how can I best avail myself of this opportunity? How can I consciously take up the inner journey along with the exoteric work involved in research?

There are many opportunities with this soul-journey, but here are a few:

Heuristic Research

Qualitative research has long recognized the value of heuristic research as valid and supportive of its methods:

> Heuristic research involves self-search, self-dialogue, and self-discovery; the research question and the methodology flow out of inner awareness, meaning and inspiration. (Moustakas, p. 11)

Often this involves journaling, meditation and reflection in general. One recent doctoral student I worked with did her research on Dream Incubation. Over time she kept track of her dreams and did extensive journaling. She also worked with the fascinating intersection of her dreams and everyday experiences she had in school and at home.

> To look at any thing
> If you would know that thing,
> You must look at it long:
> To look at this green and say,
> "I have seen a spring in these
> Woods"—will not do—you must
> Be the thing you see:
> You must be the dark snakes of
> Stems and ferny plumes of leaves,

> You must enter in
> To the small silences between
> The leaves,
> You must take your time
> And touch the very place
> They issue from.
>   (Moustakas quoting Moffitt, p. 12)

One added aspect which I cannot go into here but just want to name: When one takes the inner journey all sorts of things can be drawn forth from the deep recesses of consciousness. Sometimes those memories are painful. I sometimes have a person in tears in my class. In the context of a research course all we can do is listen, support, indicate resources and make a loving circle around the person reliving memories. If more systematic work is needed, we also recommend counseling. But for those seeking a therapeutic career path (and we have more and more research papers coming toward us on this theme), we have our Antioch TSHE and CfA Kairos Programs (see appendix, page 111).

Meditation

In various practices throughout history, those on the inner journey have worked with meditation as a rich source of personal nourishment as well as material for carrying a question. There are many avenues for doing meditation in the context of research, but here are a few I have found most helpful:

- Finding a verse or mantra that speaks to the inner condition of the question at hand and working with it over many weeks/months.

- Asking a question before sleep and then being attentive to what comes in the first moments upon waking the next day.

- Finding a place in nature to literally sit with a question.

- Doing a review of the day from the vantage point of a research question: was there anything said in a personal conversation that struck a chord? Did I see an article or view an image that spoke to my question? Did a thought come to me unexpectedly that would have flown past had I not caught it for future work with my research question?

- There are also certain movement exercises that can help promote the meditative experience.

Movement and the Inner Journey

Beginning at age three, eurythmy has been a vital part of my life. Standing in the living room of Lisa Monges, a founder of Eurythmy Spring Valley, I did simple movements accompanying poems and nursery rhymes. I really had no idea why my parents put me in that toddler eurythmy class. But the sessions were short and some of my friends were there...

As a Waldorf student, I had a love/hate relationship with eurythmy over the years, but as an adult I have come to appreciate it more and more with each year, using eurythmy in the workplace as an integral part of our CfA Waldorf Leadership Development Program, thanks to dear colleagues such as Leonore Russel and Carla Beebe Comey.

But in terms of research and the inner life, there are also many options. At a recent conference in Dornach run by young doctors, they demonstrated on the large stage one of my mother's favorite eurythmy exercises: Light streams upward, weight bears downward. They did it in terms of a medical approach to holistic healing, but I immediately saw it through the lens of personal practice and the inner life:

As one speaks the words "light streams upward" one
can extend the arms upward in a large V. Then with
"weight bears downward" one forms a V with the
legs and then follows with the arms in a downward,
upside-down V.

The doctors pointed out the importance of imagining
the movements before doing them, and the intimate
place where the two "triangles" intersect at the solar
plexis. This can be seen as step one.

But taking it further in the context of research, one can
do this exercise daily, but work with it in different ways. For
example, the light streaming upward is also an opening for
in-streaming inspiration, the true source of good teaching and
research. The light streaming downward (finding the weight
of the earth) is the "incarnation path" of taking these inspirations and actually doing something with them, such as writing.
Thus, at first glance, this movement exercise can be seen as
a whole-body experience of taking the invisible thought and
bringing it into the world as action.

But living with this basic movement exercise over time, one
can then start to elaborate further. One more example: Using
one of my favorite meditations, I have recently been doing the
"light streams upward" and "weight bears downward" gestures with alternating lines:

In my heart shines the power of the sun. (upward V)
In my soul, the warmth of the world is at work.
    (downward V, and then continuing to alternate gestures)
I breath the power of the sun.
I feel the warmth of the world. (hands crossed over heart)
May the power of the sun fill me. (V upward)
May the warmth of the world penetrate me. (downward)

Even when seated in a bus or airplane when one cannot move, if one has done the above exercise long enough with real movements, one can do a silent meditation picturing the movements, and they still work!

Using the Arts for Research and the Inner Path

In addition to eurythmy, there are many other artistic ways to explore a research question: clay modeling, painting, drawing, etc. Here the key is often the doing and then reflecting on what has been experienced. Sometimes there may seem to be little connection to the actual research question at hand, *but the artistic process itself stirs the transformative process* that is at the heart of all research journeying.

Living with the "Mystery" of the Unknown

One can start with a provocative quote from a respected author such as Rudolf Steiner and simply live with it for many days. It helps to write it on an index card and place it on one's desk or wherever one's glance can fall on it frequently throughout the day. Work with it while on a walk or before sleep. Let it become a friend. What is it saying to me? What is the language of this thought today? What was it saying to me yesterday?

Then one can try erasing it for a week. Let it go. Live in the space left by its absence. Of course, it will not really be absent, but the afterimage of the quote/thought will continue to live, and that afterimage also has a language.

Then call it back and do something with it! If painting, take up a brush and put colors on the page. For the purpose of this exercise, it does not matter what sort of image arises. Or if writing, open your laptop and start writing, mindful of the quote you have been living with.

In discussing his new passion for painting (at age 91) my father said: "If it is done out of a meditative practice it has an intention greater than me. The colors start to have a conversation that is larger than the original impulse." He gave the example of the difference between two abstract numbers, such as one plus one and two people who meet and form relationship. It is more than one plus one—sometimes it even results in the arrival of a child! The in-between becomes a presence.

Then, as a last step in this suggested process, one can reflect on the mystery of it all. How has the original quote become so large in my life? How has this actually come about? One can observe that something has started to work *through me* rather than just upon me.

Our task when following an inner path of research is to allow the content, the striving, the mystery to work through us, through and through, so that we become a vessel for something entirely new.

Working with a Mantra

Thanks to anthroposophy there are numerous verses that can be used for meditation. One can find a highly potent source in the mantra given to the School of Spiritual Science founded by Rudolf Steiner in 1923 and '24. This material has an abundance of opportunities for the seeker to go deep, and, in so doing, cross the "threshold." One can learn to work very consciously with imaginations and mantras that can help us move beyond ordinary sensory experience to see various suprasensory truths that can inform research and, indeed, one's whole life.

Research as Gifting

Some of the above opportunities can lead to a growing sense that research involves a kind of gifting. We are "endowed" with grace, given more than we ever had before. The whole effort with anthroposophically inspired research is to prepare ourselves to be ready for this gifting, to be a worthy vessel.

One tried and true method to enhance "gifting" is to work with those we have known who have died. Picturing a person we know well and who is now across the threshold, remembering a conversation, holding a personal memento, reading to the departed, all these techniques and more (see *The False Door*) can help us open pathways for them to work with us. They can give us insights (especially upon waking from sleep) and they can help us find the courage and light to pursue our destiny questions.

Finally, we need to be open to spontaneity, to the unexpected. The creative process is not just the conscious work, it also has a lot that can surface in the moment. When one opens the creative faucet in research, remarkable things can happen. We need to be open to what comes to us when we have done some of the above work and find ourselves ready to receive.

Time as a Wise Teacher

In our Waldorf summer sequence teacher education program at Antioch University, I teach a research course to entering students in their first July session. It is basically an anthroposophy course with research as a path of inquiry embedded in it. We go through a multi-week process of finding our question/topic, looking at research methods, resources, etc. as described in other sections of this pamphlet.

A great source of support to students in their research at Antioch is the arc of twelve months: the research course in July, the gathering of materials and reading in the fall, the paper writing and editing in the winter/spring, and then the presentations to the community in the next summer sessions. This length of time allows for both breadth and depth and for truly "carrying" a topic or question over time. Students are able to integrate the theme in daily living and their professional life, and find ever new ways to see the question with "beginners' eyes."

There is much that can be said about the wisdom of time, especially in an age when most of civilization is geared toward doing things faster. Rather than just Googling an answer, the twelve-month process allows for a kind of maturation that rarely occurs in academic life, let alone the sensory overload of our daily lives.

One aspect, not so frequently mentioned, is that of the four seasons in relation to the ancient wisdom of archangels. There are sources for further study on this theme, such as Steiner's *Four Seasons and the Archangels*, but here are a few leading thoughts to begin with:

> **Summer:** The stern gaze of Uriel helps us discern. Why am I here? What is my purpose in doing this professional development? Out of the many questions and possible topics, which one should I take up? With small group interactive conversations, the overprocess for several weeks, feedback from the instructor and a guided filtering process, Uriel can help us make a judgement and come to a resolve.

> **Fall:** With the return to school and home, it can be hard to stay focused on academic matters (especially since our summer sequence students are on university "vacation semester" in the fall = no tuition

LISTENING TO OUR TEACHERS

payments!). But everyone is encouraged to perse-
vere with the question taken up in the summer, do
readings and refine an outline of a future paper. This
working alone despite all odds requires the courage
and strength of Michael. His help is there for those
who ask.

Winter/spring: The impulse of Gabriel (old ways, traditions) gradually leads to Raphael, healing and transformation. A balance to Michael, the gentle support
of Raphael is needed to coax forth the thoughts
and words that are to find their way into the actual
paper.

For this winter/spring season we have long had
"journal partners" who correspond weekly, providing support and encouragement. We also have
added group zoom sessions so everyone can problem solve together, share progress reports and take
up some of the larger social justice issues of our
time (nonviolent communication, parent-teacher
relations, racialized trauma). It is important that
each of us see our *individual question/topic in relation to the world at large.* "To see the world in a
grain of sand..."

Second Summer: The culmination of the arc of
research at Antioch is community gatherings in the
Pine Hill auditorium for student presentations on
their topics. Here again, we work with the guidance of Uriel: How to share in ten to fifteen minutes the work of twelve months? What is the essential? What can be most helpful to my peers and the
other three groups listening? And most of all: what
is the essence of my learning, what has this journey
been all about? (See previous reflections from my
colleague Debbie Spitulnik.)

When done with sincerity and good will, the research process can work with the wise guidance of time and all the archangelic beings available to human beings on this earth today.

17

Why Do Research? (Revisited)

I n this section I would like to touch on a few themes, indicating areas that might prove fruitful to those looking at the research process as a matter of self-development.

Here are a few themes:

Research as a Path of Knowledge

How can I learn what I need to know in order to teach? This question is a constant companion to many a teacher. Learning and teaching walk side by side down the path of life; the one is inseparable from the other. Learning through "preparation" and learning through teaching inform one another; they create the rich tapestry we call experience.

The demands of the profession are such, however, that many teachers move from one four-course meal to another; they learn the content needed in the immediate situation, but often have little time to process the experiences. Even though the content worked with may be rich, the preparation methods consist all too often of academic habits carried over from the teacher's own undergraduate years.

How can teachers renew the art of learning? One approach is to reexamine the process of knowing, to research.

In the book *The Stages of Higher Knowledge*, Rudolf Steiner describes four phases or steps in the path of knowledge:

1. Material Knowledge
2. Imaginative Knowledge
3. Inspirational Knowledge
4. Intuitive Knowledge[33]

I would like to use this sequence to indicate how research can enhance spiritual development and intensify the process of teacher preparation. In the Waldorf model, teachers are asked to move from grade to grade, following a group of children. This necessitates a great deal of new preparation each year. It is not enough to just amass large amounts of information—good teachers learn how to process the material and transform it in age-appropriate, exciting ways, designing activities and learning experiences that awaken the curiosity and passion of their students. In order to do this "awakening," the teacher herself must be inwardly alive. Imagination, inspiration and a healthy dose of intuition go a long way in the teaching profession.

In the course of a day, we take in many sense impressions. These impressions come from objects and things around us in everyday life. Yet these sensations are meaningless without a response. We respond to the impression with our feelings, a part of our suprasensory organism called the sentient soul. In the meeting of outer sensation and soul response, consciousness is born. One can then turn away from the original sense impressions and, because of the inner activity involved in the response, an image remains. We can then "make sense" of the image by forming a "concept" out of the original image. For example, one might see a clipper ship in the harbor on July 4th, retain the image even when one turns away, but it is only when one forms the concept "ship" that one has achieved understanding. But a fourth element enters the process of material cognition, namely the organizing element of the ego. Through its activity, images and concepts are united and form the basis of memory. The image itself remains only as long as the soul is engaged in the sensory experience, but thanks to the ego, we are able to relate the impressions of today with those of the past; we are able to remember. This is the foundation of our inner life.

Also in regard to concepts, the ego engages in relational activity. It combines concepts, builds understanding, and through marvelous inner activity, helps the human being form judgments. Thus material cognition is based upon the ability to process sensations so that an image is formed, a concept arises, and is unified by the activity of the ego. The act of cognition is the basic building block of research.

At the next, higher level of cognition, the sensation from without is replaced by an image from within. This is called *imagination*. Through this faculty, images can become active for the individual that are not dependent upon physical sensation, but can be nevertheless just as vivid and true. Through meditation and other exercises one can gradually learn to form meaningful images free of sensory stimulation. Yet the process of forming concepts and the relatedness achieved by the ego remain just as important, if not more so, than before, in that one has to learn to discern real images from flights of fancy. When working with imaginative cognition, the responsibility of the researcher becomes all the greater.

In the third stage, image no longer plays a role, for now one is working just with "concept" and "ego." The human being lives wholly within the spiritual world. The stimulation of sensation in the first stage is replaced by *imagination* in the second, and *inspiration* in the third stage of cognition. One is able to actually hear the tones of the spiritual world and penetrate to the very heart of things. This is what is happening, for example, when one wakes up one morning and says, "Now I know what book I will give Ben to read."

And finally, in the fourth stage, the ego remains alone. The experience, as related by Rudolf Steiner, is that of no longer being outside things and occurrences, but now one stands within them. This living into things is called *intuition*. Then, when one is in the middle of a busy classroom, with little time for consideration of planning, suddenly one takes action, intervenes in a social situation among the children, and afterward one wonders, "Where did that come from?"

Although this book has dealt mainly with techniques on the first level of knowing, material cognition, it seems essential to describe the full process available to the student of higher knowledge. For research and self-development are, in my opinion, vitally connected. The results achieved at one level can only be fructified and enhanced by the striving of another level of insight.

In working with the above passages, it occurred to me that those engaged in research have, especially in recent years, articulated numerous avenues of inquiry that somewhat parallel the four stages just described. So, for instance, heuristic research attempts to get inside of the experience. Qualitative research accepts the role of intuition getting to the essence of the questions. Phenomenology accepts the importance of both outer and inner events as in the second stage, and traditional, quantitative research places an emphasis on what is linked to sense perceptions.

Depending upon the subject of the inquiry, those engaged in research are advised to consider not only the content but also the process that is most suitable. Do we want to look at things from the outside or from the inside? In everyday life, one usually experiences the world from outside and oneself from the inside. Research contains the possibility, if necessary, of reversing this: to experience things as if from the inside and oneself as if from outside. Knowledge of the world thus goes hand in hand with knowledge of self. And how we get there is just as important as what we find. As Emily Bowers of the Waldorf Teacher Education Program at Antioch New England says:

> While I have long had a deep love and connection with the French language, my research enabled me to penetrate the "genius of the language." With a better understanding of the development of the French language, I came upon the greater revelation of the evolution of human speech— speech in its highest glory and darkest hour.

One also has to start somewhere. So often teachers shy away from even the thought of research, and thus I have tried to address research on a simple, "first steps" basis, in the hopes that some new activity is stimulated. Part of the challenge is simply organizing ourselves, learning how to ask the question, observe, collect and share. But I hope the process is both internal and external; that self-development goes hand in hand with strengthening connections between schools and teachers. A research collaborative can do for education what farmers' markets have done for local villages in New England. We need to grow our standards organically rather than importing solutions that don't fit. Sharing teacher research projects can help educators be proactive in setting the agenda rather than always responding to outside mandates. A community of enthusiastic teachers can bring back a sense of neighborhood schools and of community. A stronger voice for the local community will push back against state and federal legislation. And in the end, the only ones "left behind" may be the old-style politicians who care more about their campaign donations than about the needs of real children. The best thing about democracy is the possibility of civic action. It is time for teachers and parents to speak out, for *they know* what their children need most.

18

The Uncertainty Principle in Research

From *Sand Talk: How Indigenous Thinking Can Save the World* by Tyson Yunkaporta:

No matter how hard you may try to separate yourself from reality, there are always observer effects as the reality shifts in relation to your viewpoint. Scientists call this the uncertainty principle. (pp. 40–41)

From an Aboriginal cosmological point of view, the uncertainty problem is resolved when you admit you are part of the field and accept your subjectivity....

Scientists currently have to remove all traces of themselves from experiments, otherwise their data is considered to be contaminated. Contaminated with what? With the filthy reality of belongingness? The toxic realization that if we can't stand outside of a field, we can't own it? I don't see science embracing Indigenous methods of inquiry anytime soon, as Indigenous Knowledge is not wanted at the level *of how,* only at the level of *what,* a resource to be plundered rather than a source of knowledge processes. *Show me where some plants are so I can synthesize a compound and make drugs out of it.* (p. 42)

19

The Use of AI for Teacher Research

Thanks to my colleague Sage Lewis, I have started to wade into the "new terrain" of AI and the many possibilities (and potential pitfalls) of harnessing this new tool for teacher research. He recently shared the following:

> Here is what ChatGPT thinks about the topic: The integration of Artificial Intelligence (AI) into educational research, particularly for Waldorf teachers, opens up a myriad of possibilities and implications that could significantly enhance the depth and breadth of pedagogical studies. Waldorf education, with its emphasis on holistic development, artistic expression, and experiential learning, presents a unique context for AI applications. AI can assist Waldorf teachers in conducting research by providing advanced data analysis tools that uncover patterns and insights within educational outcomes, learning behaviors, and the effectiveness of teaching methodologies. This could lead to more personalized learning experiences, enabling teachers to tailor their approaches to the individual needs of each student, while still adhering to the core principles of Waldorf education.
>
> Moreover, AI technologies can facilitate access to a vast array of academic resources and literature, streamlining the research process for teachers who are exploring innovative teaching practices or looking to integrate interdisciplinary studies into their curriculum. However, it's crucial to approach the integration of AI with caution,

ensuring that technology supports rather than detracts from the human-centric and nature-oriented ethos of Waldorf education. The challenge lies in leveraging AI to enhance educational research and practice while preserving the essence of Waldorf education that values human interaction, creativity, and the development of the whole child. As Waldorf educators navigate this new terrain, the possibilities for enriching educational research and outcomes through AI are vast, yet they must be balanced with a thoughtful consideration of the implications for the educational philosophy they uphold.

Sage continues:

Personally, AI has deepened my understanding of Steiner's desire to find proof of the spiritual. AI finally made me get it. Like, get it all.

Ever since Guttenburg, we have used technology to get closer to God. Imagine that day you got a Bible in your house and could read God's word for yourself. How empowering!

AI is like that. It is total access to all written thoughts from all time. Within these words, I believe, is the proof of God. AI democratizes ALL information.

And as ChatGPT warns, we must be aware that it has the potential to drive some of us into a more material, less spiritual world. But it is the Waldorf teachers who must guide the world in the direction of increased spiritual understanding.

I genuinely believe AI is the tool that will increase spiritual practice when it is understood for its true meaning.

I asked ChatGPT this: What do you think Rudolf Steiner would have thought about the advent of AI?

Here is its response:

Rudolf Steiner, the founder of Anthroposophy and the Waldorf education system, held views deeply rooted in the development of human consciousness and spiritual science. Given his emphasis on the importance of human intuition, creativity, and spiritual development, Steiner might have approached the advent of Artificial Intelligence (AI) with a mix of caution and interest.

On one hand, Steiner might have seen the potential of AI to contribute to society in ways that free individuals from mundane tasks, allowing them more time and energy to pursue spiritual growth, artistic endeavors, and the development of their inner selves—core aspects of his philosophy. He could have appreciated the ways in which AI can support human learning, especially if it enables a more personalized and holistic educational approach, aligning with his views on teaching and learning.

On the other hand, Steiner would likely express concerns about the implications of AI on human consciousness and spiritual freedom. He might worry that over-reliance on AI could lead to a diminishment of human capacities, such as critical thinking, empathy, and creativity, which are essential for the spiritual evolution he advocated. Steiner's emphasis on the importance of direct human experiences, interpersonal relationships, and engagement with the natural world could lead him to caution against technologies that might isolate individuals or reduce their engagement in these areas.

Ultimately, Steiner would probably have encouraged a thoughtful and conscious approach to the integration of AI into society, emphasizing the need to balance technological advancement with the cultivation of human values and spiritual development. He might advocate for the development of AI in ways that support and enhance human capabilities, rather than replace them, ensuring that technology serves humanity's higher spiritual and moral goals.

And a footnote from me: As with all research, we need to continually monitor the quality of our sources and where they come from. It is the same with AI.

In a March 19, 2024, *Wall Street Journal* article, Jackie Snow describes the potential for "data poisoning": "While data poisoning is a concern with all types of machine-learning algorithms, some researchers say generative AI models could be particularly vulnerable because they must ingest vast amounts of text, imagery and other data from the public internet to gain the knowledge they need to create something on their own"(*WSJ* p. R4). As I understand her, it is not AI in itself that is the issue, but rather the potential (as in other situations) for hackers to intentionally pollute the articles or information just before they are uploaded into Wikipedia, for example. Fortunately, there is a growing global community of volunteers who curate the content of online sources and form a first line of defense against content manipulation.

As with so many advances in technology over the past decades, AI is an opportunity both for teacher research and for heightened understanding and wakefulness in this age of the consciousness soul.

20

Research as Teacher Empowerment

This is a natural result of the research process. As we intensify our observations, gain understanding as well as self-knowledge, reflect on practice and learn to better articulate what we are doing, we can experience a new kind of professional and personal freedom. This can lead to new roles in educational leadership and community activism as described earlier.

Research as Renewal

One might simply take up the theme of stress transformation. Find something that bothers you, and then make it your research question. It is amazing what happens when a source of frustration is brought under observation and study for a period of time. When I became concerned about teacher burnout, I started to observe the phenomenon in myself and in others, and I finally took it up as a research project that culminated in my second book, *School Renewal.*

Research and Professional Development

If we as teachers are actively engaged in learning through research, our students benefit immediately. Our involvement, even if not on grade level material, acts as a quickening element in their learning. Our vitality and enthusiasm directly affect the participation and health of the children. In the schools I have observed, those teachers who are "fired up," enthusiastic and engaging are often those who are most actively engaged in the discovery process themselves. They are seeing things with "new eyes" and bringing a fresh simplicity to their work with children.

Research as a Deepening of Education

On September 6, 1919, at the end of his address to the teachers of the first Waldorf school in Stuttgart, Rudolf Steiner called attention to something that he wanted to lay upon the hearts of the teachers present. These simple principles are as important for teachers today as they were back in 1919:

> The teacher must be a person of initiative in everything he or she does, great and small.
> The teacher should be one who is interested in the being of the whole world and of humanity.
> The teacher must be one who never makes a compromise in his or her heart and mind with what is untrue.
> The teacher must never get stale or grow sour.[34]

If one lives with these four statements and the text that accompanies them in a book called the *Deepening of Waldorf Education*, one cannot but see the relevance of teacher-inspired research.

Teachers now need to take initiative, become "authors" in the larger sense. Research affords us an opportunity to accept the challenge of the age of the consciousness soul, pass through the eye of the needle, and come through our experiences as individuals who speak with a new voice. This next stage of our work is not a luxury; it is a necessity if we are to counter NCLB and other government mandates. The creative forces that may be released from enchantment, if teacher research is truly taken up, cannot be fully imagined. It all begins with the response of each individual to this call. Let me end with a passage from *Leaves of Grass* by Walt Whitman:

> You shall no longer take things at second or third hand,
> Nor look through the eyes of the dead,
> > nor feed on the specters of books,
> You shall not look through my eyes either,
> > nor take things from me,
> You shall listen to all sides and filter them from
> > yourself.[35]

Appendices

1. A Metaphor

The following is a metaphor that could be used for the research process as well as for soup!

Soulful Soup

A Recipe by Erin Geesaman Rabke

You'll need:

1. Space in your heart-mind
2. Several excellent questions and insights
3. The heat of your affection
4. A hefty dose of curiosity
5. And unhurried time.

Directions:

- First, find the big stock pot or cauldron that lives in your imagination. Make sure it's not over-full with exhausting information you do not need to know. Wash it out, rinse it, dry it, and then...

- Add this fresh question from Zen teacher Scott Morrison: *Do I wish to live this moment with as much attention, care, and affection as possible or am I going to do something else?* (There's no point in judging the something else as good or bad—it's just good to know who's making the decision.)

- Heat gently with the warmth of your affection for life. You may need to blow on the embers to really get the heat going. Don't give up. The fire can be kindled.

- Once that first question is sizzling, stir in Michael Meade's potent life-reflection question: *Did you become yourself?*

- When those two questions soften together, after a few minutes, gently stir in this question: *What do I need to do to deepen my self respect?*

- Add in a gentle reminder of the world's problems mixed with what's weighing heavy on your heart. (Just the right amount of bitter flavor brings out the complexity in a delicious way.)

- Add water to cover.

- As you stir in the water, remind yourself of this wisdom from the *Tao Te Ching*: *Nothing in the world is as soft and yielding as water. Yet for dissolving the hard and inflexible, nothing can surpass it.*

- When you start to recognize the scent of your own curiosity, grounded and engaged, gently add this directive from the late, great Barry Lopez: *We must invent overnight, figuratively speaking, another kind of civilization, one more cognizant of limits, less greedy, more compassionate, less bigoted, more inclusive, less exploitive.*

- Notice creative ideas and inspiration rising in the steam. Breathe it in deeply.

- Add this potent reminder from Francis Weller: *The task of a mature human being is to carry grief in one hand and gratitude in the other and to be stretched large by them.*

- Yum.

- Bring to a simmer.

- Simmering can happen as you walk, as you sit in your favorite chair, or even in the shower.

- Simmer for a good long while.

- When the time feels right, add this ingredient from Kathleen Dean Moore: *It doesn't matter what it is. If it's generous to life, imagine it into existence.*

- Once that has dissolved into the savory broth, take a pinch of impermanence and sprinkle over the top. Remind yourself that all of this—the beauty, the beings, the pains-in-the-ass, will not last. Who knows how long you have left in this body, on this earth? Notice how this recognition changes the flavor of everything.

- More vibrant, brighter even. This is good.

- Then season to taste with Mary Oliver's salt, which she labels the *"only one question"* to ask: *How to love this world?*

- Salt makes things tasty and this kind won't raise your blood pressure. Be generous.

- And if you like spice, add a pinch of this advice from Desmond Tutu: *Free yourself. Free others. Serve everyday.*

- Top with a generous drizzle of this extra virgin inquiry: *How can I make this whole endeavor less effortful and more pleasurable? Even beautiful?*

- Then grate over the top this reminder from Thinley Norbu: *Serious mind is always exhausted.*

- Play mind always has energy.

- Serve it up in a favorite bowl.

- Sip this stew regularly. Chew on it daily. Share it with those you love.

- It's revolutionary, liberatory, deeply nutritious, and anti-inflammatory. If you make it with love, it's bound to be delicious and with a unique flavor only you could create.

- Enjoy!

2. Kairos: Healing in a World of Need

Karine Munk Finser

This spring (2024), with the total solar eclipse on April 8th following the lunar eclipse on March 25th, we are especially aware of these cosmic signatures and turn toward the heavens, the cosmic source of all life.

If we are the microcosm, then these larger movements of the macrocosm surely affect us and speak of both the solar and lunar paths being hindered, as the sources of light and reflected light are cut off from us for a time.

We can see in these events images of the strongest light juxtaposed with the strongest darkness.

The moon has always been associated with the sacred vessel, the grail, and serves as the cosmic mirror of the body. The human body can also experience an eclipse and be hindered under certain circumstances.

When we are exposed to too much too soon—to extreme trauma or cumulative smaller trauma, to man-made or natural disasters, to catastrophic hunger or land displacement—the danger of no longer feeling safe in one's own body becomes a reality that, if not naturally healed or addressed, may cause a serious interruption in a person's destiny path.

Many children and young people who suffer trauma are experiencing an eclipse of their essential selves. It lasts for much longer than minutes, as their bodily vessel is no longer able to work with the incarnating "I"-forces.

There is a disconnect which, if not addressed and helped, can prevent a normal unfolding of their lives in accordance with their pre-birth life intentions.

These kinds of soul eclipses are dangerous. Not just for the individual but for all of us. When so many suffer a separation from the genius of their lives, we all suffer. The creativity and healing of many of our challenges here on earth depend on the health of one another.

Orland Bishop said it best in one of our Kairos Sessions: "Only I-beings truly meet." When we are allowed to unfold our integrity and dignity as human beings, our I am can find its home in the warmth of our bodies and in our will forces.

This makes it possible for us to unfold our individual creativity, bringing more light into our world.

The mission of Kairos Institute is to share pedagogical and artistic practices that bring healing to those whose destiny has been impacted by traumatic events.

Following a celestial eclipse, we rejoice together at the return of the light; in the sphere of human destiny, when the suffering of young people is lifted, freeing them from the shadow of events, we rejoice that their gifts can be shared anew.

Kairos Institute and Center for Anthroposophy:

https://centerforanthroposophy.org/programs/kairos-institute/

3. World Social Initiative in Transition

Joan Sleigh

The World Social Initiative Forum (WSIF) promotes independence in local cultural contexts. The team is now returning the stewardship of the projects to the Section for Social Sciences, from where it will be passed on to the new Section for Inclusive Social Development.

The World Social Initiative Forum (WSIF), founded in 2000 through the initiative of Ute Craemer and Truus Geraets (1930–2023) has become a global network of spiritually inspired individuals and organizations that foster social equity and diversity within local groupings, to connect as a global multicultural society.

Building Bridges

"'Bridge-building' was and continues to be our motto," says Ute Craemer:

> Bridging between the grassroots and the financial worlds, between anthroposophy and indigenous cultures, between the life dreams of young people living in slums and the youth living in gated communities, between the spiritual and the earthly worlds.

And Truus Geraets always used to say, "We also hope for close cooperation with all the sections at the Goetheanum and individuals from multi-ethnic projects—that all voices may be heard in dialogue."

As a project of the Section for Social Sciences at the Goetheanum the WSIF Team consisted of six young individuals, led by Joan Sleigh. Since 2015, WSIF has hosted multiple forums: in Asia (India 2016 and Japan 2018); in Europe (Switzerland 2018–2019 and 2021, U.K. 2023); in South America (Brazil 2019, Argentina 2023); in North America (U.S. 2022), and Africa (Egypt 2019 and Kenya 2024).

World Social Initiative Forum in Kenya in 2024
Photo: Nicole Asis)

Each WSIF Forum promoted the free unfolding of individual potential, nurtured genuine interest in others, supported an economy that serves the needs of all and engaged in care for the earth as a living organism. The events addressed the sociocultural challenges relevant to the different places, by cohosting interactive dialogues, practices and communal learning.

The work of the WSIF transitioned online at the onset of the Covid pandemic. This enabled local dialogues and sociopolitical challenges to be explored on a global basis, resulting in the development of a multicultural research community. The events fostered trust and empathy, ignited the unfolding of individual agency, and supported fluid transformation towards healthy community living in which each individual is acknowledged in his or her own uniqueness.

WSIF has become an associative network of individuals and enterprises woven around the School of Spiritual Science by promoting anthroposophy-in-dialogue—drawing sustenance from the spirit of anthroposophy, while offering the resilience and cohesion of the ancient indigenous spirit of the place where the Forums are hosted, as well as acknowledging its current context and its social questions, needs and abundance.

More Regional Independence

During the last two years, WSIF could once again co-host forums on the ground which has resulted in the work being taken up and continued in regional networks in the UK, in Latin America and in East Africa. These now join the existing regional SIF in Egypt and Japan.

In celebration of WSIF's coming-of-age and moving into independent regions, as well as due to individual biographical changes in the WSIF Team, the stewardship of the WSIF projects and network will now transition back into the umbrella of the Section for Social Sciences at the Goetheanum. In agreement with the WSIF Advisory Board it will remain there until the new Section for Inclusive Social Development will have established itself enough to host the WSIF Network as an active collaborative partner.

Joan Sleigh, born 1962 in Hermanus (SA), is a Waldorf teacher and former lecturer at the Centre for Creative Education. From 2013 to 2020, she was a member of the General Anthroposophical Society's Executive Council at the Goetheanum. She is currently project manager at the Social Initiative Forum.

4. Alternative Question Formats

Special thanks to Michael Patton
for much of the material in the following appendices

Dichotomous lead-in questions	Presupposition lead-in questions
Do you feel like you know enough about the program to assess its effectiveness?	How effective do you think the program is? (Presupposes that a judgment can be made)
Have you learned anything from this program?	What have you learned from this program? (Presupposes learning)
Do you do anything now in your work that you didn't do before the program began?	What do you do now that you didn't do before the program began? (Presupposes change)
Is there any misuse of funds in this program?	What kinds of misuse of funds have occurred in this program? (Presupposes at least some misuse of funds)
Are there any conflicts among the staff?	What kinds of staff conflicts have occurred here? (Presupposes conflicts)

5. Fieldwork Strategies and Observation Methods

I. ROLE OF THE EVALUATOR-OBSERVER

FULL   **ONLOOKER**

Participant observation   Partial observation   Observation as an outsider

II. PORTRAYAL OF THE EVALUATOR ROLE TO OTHERS

OVERT   **COVERT**

| Observations: Program staff and participants know that observations are being made or who the observer is | Observer: Role known by some, not by others | Observations: Program staff and participants do not know that others are present as observers |

III. PORTRAYAL OF THE PURPOSE OF THE EVALUATION TO OTHERS

| Full explanation of real purpose to everyone | Partial explanations | Covert explanations: None given to either staff or participants | False explanations: Staff and particpants deceived about evaluation purpose |

IV. DURATION OF THE EVALUATION OBSERVATIONS

Single observation: Limited duration (e.g., one hour)

Long-term, multiple observations (e.g., months, years)

V. FOCUS OF THE OBSERVATIONS

NAROW FOCUS   **BROAD FOCUS**

Single element or component in the program observed

Holistic view of the entire program and all of its elements

6. Interviews

| WHAT THE INTERVIEWER REALLY WANTED TO KNOW: OPEN-ENDED QUESTION:
--- | ---
Q: Were you the evaluator of this program? | What was your role in this program?
A: Yes. |
Q: Were you doing a formative evaluation? | What was the purpose of the evaluation?
A: Mostly. |
Q: Were you trying to find out if the people changed from being in the wilderness? | What were you trying to find out in doing the evaluation?
A: That was part of it. |
Q: Did they change? | How did participation in the program affect participants?
A: Some of them did. |
Q: Did you interview people both before and after the program? | What kinds of information did you collect for the evaluation?
A: Yes. |
Q: Did you also go along as a participant in the program? | How were you personally involved in the program?
A: Yes. |
Q: Did you find that being in the program affected what happened? | How do you think your participation in the program affected what happened?
A: Yes. |
Q: Did you have a good time? | What was the wilderness experience like for you?
A: Yes. |

VAGUE AND OVERGENERALIZED NOTES:	DETAILED AND CONCRETE NOTES:
1. The new client was uneasy waiting for her intake interview.	1. At first the new client sat very stiffly on the chair next to the receptionist's desk. She picked up a magazine and let the pages flutter through her fingers very quickly without really looking at any of the pages. She set the magazine down, looked at her watch, tugged at her skirt, and picked up the magazine again. This time she didn't look at the magazine. She set it back down, took out a cigarette, and began smoking. She would watch the receptionist out of the corner of her eye, and then look down at the magazine, and back up at the two or three other people waiting in the room. Her eyes moved from the people to the magazine to the cigarette to the people to the magazine in rapid succession. She avoided eye contact. When her name was finally called she jumped as if she was startled.
2. The client was quite hostile toward the staff person.	2. When Judy, the senior staff member, told her that she could not do what she wanted to do, the client began to yell at Judy, telling her that she couldn't control her life, that she was on nothing but a "power trip," that she'd "like to beat the shit out of her," and that she could just "go to hell." She shook her fist in Judy's face and stomped out of the room, leaving Judy standing there with her mouth open, looking amazed.
3. The next student who came in to take the test was very poorly dressed	3. The next student who came into the room was wearing clothes quite different from the three students who'd been in previously. The three previous students looked like they'd been groomed before they came to the test. Their hair was combed, their clothes were clean and pressed, the colors of their clothes matched, and their clothes were in good condition. This new student had on pants that were dirty, with a hole or tear in one knee and a threadbare seat. The flannel shirt was wrinkled, with one tail tucked into the pants and the other tail hanging out. His hair was disheveled, and his hands looked as though he'd been playing in the engine of a car.

7. Variety in Qualitative Inquiry: Theoretical Traditions

PERSPECTIVE:	DISCIPLINARY ROOTS:	CENTRAL QUESTIONS:
1. Ethnography	Anthropology	What is the culture of this group of people?
2. Phenomenology	Philosophy	What is the structure and essence of experience of this phenomenon for these people?
3. Heuristics	Humanistic psychology	What is my experience of this phenomenon and the essential experience of others who also experience this phenomenon intensely?
4. Ethnomethodology	Sociology	How do people make sense of their everyday activities so as to behave in socially acceptable ways?
5. Symbolic interactionism	Social psychology	What common set of symbols and understandings have emerged to give meaning to people's interactions?
6. Ecological psychology	Ecology, Psychology	How do individuals attempt to accomplish their goals through specific behaviors in specific environments?
7. Systems theory	Interdisciplinary	How and why does this system function as a whole?
8. Chaos theory: nonlinear interaction	Theoretical physics, Natural sciences	What is the underlying order, if any, of disorderly phenomena?
9. Hermeneutics	Theology, Philosophy, Literary criticism	What are the conditions under which a human act took place or a product was produced that makes it possible to interpret its meanings?
10. Orientational, qualitative	Ideologies, Political economy	How is x ideological perspective manifest in this phenomenon?

8. Typology of Research Purposes

Types of Research	Purpose	Focus of Research	Desired Results
Basic research	Knowledge as an end in itself; discover truth	Questions deemed important by one's discipline or personal intellectual interest	Contribution to theory
Applied research	Understand the nature and sources of human and societal problems	Questions deemed important by society	Contributions to theories that can be used to formulate problem-solving programs and interventions
Summative evaluation	Determine effectiveness of human interventions and actions (programs, policies, personnel, and products)	Goals of intervention	Judgments and generalizations about effective types of interventions and the conditions under which those efforts are effective
Formative evaluation	Improve an intervention, a program, policy, organization, or product	Strengths and weaknesses of the specific program, policy, or personnel being studied	Recommendations for limited improvements
Action research	Solve problems in a program, organization, or community	Organization and community problems	Immediate action; solving problems as quickly as possible

Desired Level of Generalization	Key Assumptions	Publication Mode	Standard for Judging
Across time and space (ideal)	The world is patterned; those patterns are knowable and explainable	Major refereed scholarly journals in one's discipline, scholarly books	Rigor of research, universality and verifiability of theory
Within as general a time and space as possible, but clearly limited application context	Human and societal problems can be understood and solved with knowledge	Specialized academic journals, applied research journals within disciplines, interdisciplinary problem-focused journals	Rigor and theoretical insight into the problem
All interventions with similar goals	What works one place under specified conditions should work elsewhere	Evaluation reports for program funders and policy makers, specialized journals	Generalizability to future efforts and to other programs and policy issues
Limited to specific setting studied	People can and will use information to improve what they're doing	Oral briefings, conferences, internal report, limited circulation to similar programs, other evaluators	Usefulness to and actual use by intended users in the setting studied
Here and now	People in a setting can solve problems by studying themselves	Interpersonal Interactions among research participants; informal, unpublished	Feelings about the process among research participants, feasibility of the solution generated

9. Sampling Strategies

Types	Purposes
A. Random probability sampling	Representativeness: Sample size a function of population size and desired confidence level.
1. simple random sample	Permits generalization from sample to the population it represents.
2. stratified random and cluster samples	Increases confidence in generalizing to particular subgroups or areas.
B. Purposeful sampling	Selects information-rich cases for in-depth study. Size and specific cases depend on study purpose.
1. extreme or deviant case sampling	Learning from highly unusual manifestations of the phenomenon of interest, such as outstanding successes/notable failures, top of the class/ dropouts, exotic events, and crises.
2. intensity sampling	Information-rich cases that manifest the phenomenon intensely, but not extremely, such as good students/poor students, about average/below average.
3. maximum variation sampling—purposefully picking a wide range of variation on dimensions of interest	Documents unique or diverse variations that have emerged in adapting to different conditions. Identifies important common patterns that cut across variations.
4. homogeneous sampling	Focuses, reduces variation, simplifies analysis, and facilitates group interviewing.
5. typical case sampling	Illustrates or highlights what is typical, normal, and average.
6. stratified purposeful sampling	Illustrates characteristics of particular subgroups of interest; facilitates comparisons.

7. critical case sampling	Permits logical generalization and maximum application of information to other cases because if it's true of this one case, it's likely to be true of all other cases.
TYPES	*PURPOSES*
8. snowball or chain sampling	Identifies cases of interest from people who know people who know people who know what cases are information-rich, that is, good examples for study, good interview subjects.
9. criterion sampling	Picking all cases that meet some criterion, such as all children abused in a treatment facility. Quality assurance.
10. theory-based or operational construct sampling	Finding manifestations of a theoretical construct of interest to elaborate and examine the construct.
11. confirming and disconfirming cases	Elaborating and deepening initial analysis, seeking exceptions, testing variation.
12. opportunistic sampling	Following new leads during fieldwork, taking advantage of the unexpected, flexibility.
13. random purposeful sampling (still small sample size)	Adds credibility to sample when potential purposeful sample is larger than one can handle. Reduces judgment within a purposeful category (not for generalizations or representations).
14. sampling politically important cases	Attracts attention to the study (or avoids attracting undesired attention by purposefully eliminating from the sample politically sensitive cases).
15. convenience sampling	Saves time, money, and effort. Poorest rationale; lowest credibility. Yields information-poor cases.
16. combination or mixed purposeful sampling	Triangulation, flexibility, meets multiple interests and needs.

10. Design Issues and Options

Issues	Sample Options and Considerations
1. What is the primary purpose of the study?	Basic research, applied research, summative evaluation, formative evaluation, action research.
2. What is the focus of the study?	Breadth versus depth trade-offs.
3. What are the units of analysis?	Individuals, groups, program components, whole programs, organizations, communities, critical incidents, time periods, and so on.
4. What will be the sampling strategy or strategies?	Purposeful sampling, probability sampling; variations in sample size from a single case study to generalizable samples.
5. What types of data will be collected?	Qualitative, quantitative, or both.
6. What controls will be exercised?	Naturalistic inquiry, experimental design, quasi-experimental options.
7. What analytical approach or approaches will be used?	Inductive analysis, deductive content analysis, statistical analysis, combinations.

8. How will validity of and confidence in findings be addressed?	Triangulation options, multiple data sources, multiple methods, multiple perspectives, and multiple investigators.
9. Time issues: When will the study occur? How will the study be sequenced or phased?	Long-term fieldwork, rapid reconnaissance, exploratory phase to confirmatory phase, fixed times versus open time lines.
10. How will logistics and practicalities be handled?	Gaining entry to the setting, access to people and records, contracts, training, endurance, and so on.
11. How will ethical issues and matters of confidentiality be handled?	Informed consent, protection of human subjects, reactivity, presentation of self, and so on.
12. What resources will be available? What will the study cost?	Personnel, supplies, data collection, materials, analysis time and costs, reporting/publishing costs.

11. Variations in Interview Instrumentation

Type of Interview	Characteristics
(1) Informal conversational approach	Questions emerge from the immediate context and are asked in the natural course of things; there is no predetermination of question topics in wording.
(2) Interview guide approach	Topics and issues to be covered are specified in advance, in outline form; interviewer decides sequence and wording of questions in the course of the interview.
(3) Standardized open-ended interview	The exact wording and sequence of questions are determined in advance. All interviewees are asked the same basic questions in the same order. Questions are worded in a completely open-ended format.
(4) Closed, fixed response interview	Questions and response categories are determined in advance. Responses are fixed; respondent chooses from among the fixed responses.

STRENGTHS	WEAKNESSES
Increases the salience and relevance of questions; interviews are built on and emerge from observations; the interview can be matched to individuals and circumstances.	Different information collected from different people with different questions. Less systematic and comprehensive if certain questions do not arise "naturally." Data organization and analysis can be quite difficult.
The outline increases the comprehensiveness of the data and makes data collection somewhat systematic for each respondent. Logical gaps in data can be anticipated and closed. Interviews remain fairly conversational and situational.	Important and salient topics may be inadvertently omitted. Interviewer flexibility in sequencing and wording questions can result in substantially different responses from different perspectives, thus reducing the comparability of responses.
Respondents answer the same questions, thus increasing comparability of responses; data are complete for each person on the topics addressed in the interview. Reduces interviewer effects and bias when several interviewers are used. Permits evaluation users to see and review the instrumentation used in the evaluation. Facilitates organization and analysis of the data.	Little flexibility in relating the interview to particular individuals and circumstance; standardized wording of questions may constrain and limit naturalness and relevance of questions and answers.
Data analysis is simple; responses can be directly compared and easily aggregated; many questions can be asked in a short time.	Respondents must fit their experiences and feelings into the researcher's categories; may be perceived as impersonal, irrelevant, and mechanistic. Can distort what respondents really mean or experienced by so completely limiting their response choices.

Notes

1   *Educational Leadership,* Nov. 2006, vol. 64, no. 3, 10.

2   Fordham Institute, 4.

3   Ibid.

4   Susan Ohanian, *One Size Fits Few: The Folly of Educational Standards,* 4.

5   Ibid.

6   John Gardner, *Freedom and the Independent School.*

7   Rudolf Steiner, *The Renewal of the Social Organism,* 73.

8   Ibid., 73.

9   Glenda Bissex, from a guest appearance at Antioch New England, 1994.

10   David Hopkins, *A Teacher's Guide to Classroom Research,* 29.

11   Power and Hubbard, "Teacher Research," *The Journal of Classroom Inquiry,* vol. 1. 72.

12   David Hopkins, *A Teacher's Guide to Classroom Research,* 33.

13   Power and Hubbard, "Teacher Research," 67.

14   David Hopkins, *A Teacher's Guide to Classroom Research,* 48.

15   Ibid., 3.

16   Michael Patton, *Qualitative Evaluation and Research Methods.*

17   Power and Hubbard, "Teacher Research," 79.

18   Theodore Sizer, *Horace's Compromise,* 99–100.

19   David Hopkins, *A Teacher's Guide to Classroom Research,* 46.

20   Power and Hubbard, "Teacher Research," 75.

21   Jon Wagner, "Ignorance in Educational Research Or, How Can You Not Know That?," in *Educational Research,* vol. 22, no 5, 15–23.

22   Harry F. Wolcott, *Writing Up Qualitative Research,* 31.

23   Power and Hubbard, "Teacher Research," 82.

24   This chapter draws from Joseph A. Maxwell, *Qualitative Research Design: An Interactive Approach* (Applied Social Research Methods no. 41), 2nd ed., SAGE, 2004.

25   Harry F. Wolcott, *Writing Up Qualitative Research*, 35–39.

26   Patton, 150.

27   Joeliee Seed-Pihama, "Naming Our Names and Telling Our Stories," in J. Archibald, *Decolonizing Research*, 91.

28   Laurel Richardson and Elizabeth Adams St. Pierre, "Writing, A Method of Inquiry," in N. K. Denizin and Y. S. Lincoln (eds.), *The SAGE Handbook of Qualitative Research*, 818f.

29   Harry F. Wolcott, *Writing Up Qualitative Research*, 21.

30   Waldorf Teacher Education and Transdisciplinary Studies in Healing Education programs.

31   Jon Wagner, *Educational Research*, 20.

32   Power and Hubbard, "Teacher Research," 74.

33   Rudolf Steiner, *The Stages of Higher Knowledge*, 2f.

34   Rudolf Steiner, *Towards the Deepening of Waldorf Education*, 26–27.

35   Walt Whitman, *Leaves of Grass*, 50.

Bibliography

American Psychological Association (2020). *Publication manual of the American Psychological Association* (7th ed.) (https://doi.org /10.1037/0000165-000).

Archibald, J. (Q'um Q'um Xiiem), J. B. J. Lee-Morgan, J. De Santolo. (2023). *Decolonizing Research: Indigenous Storywork as Methodology*. London: Bloomsbury.

Argyris, C. (1993). *Knowledge for Action: A Guide to Overcoming Barriers to Organizational Change*. San Francisco: Jossey-Bass.

Creswell, J. W. (1994). *Research Design: Qualitative and Quantitative Approaches*. Thousand Oaks, CA: SAGE.

Denizin, N. K., and Y. S. Lincoln (eds.). (2018). *The SAGE Handbook of Qualitative Research*. Thousand Oaks, CA: SAGE.

"Educational Leadership" (2006). *64*(3). Thomas B. Fordham Institute: The Education Gadfly (URL no longer available).

Finser, T. M. (2007). *Silence Is Complicity: A Call to Let Teachers Improve Our Schools through Action Research—Not NCLB*. Great Barrington, MA: SteinerBooks.

Friere, P. (1990). *Pedagogy of the Oppressed*. New York: Continuum International.

Gardner, J. F. (1966). *Towards a Truly Public Education: A Philosophy of Independence for Schools*. Great Barrington, MA: The Myrin Institute.

—— (1975). *The Next Step*. Great Barrington, MA: The Myrin Institute.

—— (1975). *Freedom and the Independent School*. Great Barrington, MA: The Myrin Institute.

—— (1975). *Freedom for Education*. Great Barrington, MA: The Myrin Institute.

Hopkins, D. (1985). *Teacher's Guide to Classroom Research*. Milton Keynes, UK: Open University.

The Journal of Classroom Inquiry vol. 1 (1994). Albany, NY: The Johnson Press.

Maxwell, J. A. (2004). *Qualitative Research Design: An Interactive Approach*. 2nd ed. Thousand Oaks, CA: SAGE.

Mishler, E. G. (1991). *Research Interviewing: Context and Narrative.* Cambridge, MA: Harvard University.

Moustakas, C. (1990). *Heuristic Research: Design, Methodology, and Applications.* Thousand Oaks, CA: SAGE.

Ohanian, S. (1999). *One Size Fits Few: The Folly of Educational Standards.* Heinemann.

Patton, M. Q. (1990). *Qualitative Evaluation and Research Methods.* Thousand Oaks, CA: SAGE.

Richardson, L. (2018). "Writing, a Method of Inquiry." In *The SAGE Handbook of Qualitative Research.* Edited by N. K. Denizin and Y. S. Lincoln. Thousand Oaks, CA: SAGE.

Shagoury Hubbard, R., and B. Miller Power (1993). *The Art of Classroom Inquiry: A Handbook for Teacher-Reseaches.* Portsmouth, NH: Heinemann.

Sizer, T. R. (2004). *Horace's Compromise: The Dilemma of the American High School.* New York: Houghton Mifflin.

Steiner, R. (1981). *Spiritual Research: Methods and Results.* New York: Steinerbooks, Garber Communications.

—— (2017). *Towards the Deepening of Waldorf Education.* Waldorf Publications, Pedagogical Section Council.

—— (1985). *The Renewal of the Social Organism.* Spring Valley, NY: Anthroposophic Press.

—— (2009) *The Stages of Higher Knowledge: Imagination, Inspiration, Intuition.* 2nd ed. Great Barrington, MA: SteinerBooks.

Stoff, S. P. (1977). "Freedom and Independence in Education." New York: Council for Educational Freedom in America. *The Research Bulletin,* Hudson, NY: Research Institute for Waldorf Education, 2006, 12(1).

Whitman, W. (1955). *Leaves of Grass.* New York: Signet Classic, New American Library.

Wagner, J., et al. (1993). "Ignorance in Educational Research Or, How Can You Not Know That?" *SAGE Journals* (https://journals.sagepub.com/doi/10.3102/0013189X022005015).

Wolcott, H. F. (1990). *Writing Up Qualitative Research.* Thousand Oaks, CA: SAGE.

Yunkaporta, T. (2020). *Sand Talk: How Indigenous Thinking Can Save the World.* New York: HarperCollins.

www.ingramcontent.com/pod-product-compliance
Lightning Source LLC
Chambersburg PA
CBHW021008090426
42738CB00007B/707